MEETING
St. Mark
TODAY

MEETING
St. Mark
TODAY

Understanding the Man,
His Mission, and His Message

DANIEL J. HARRINGTON, SJ

LOYOLA PRESS.
A JESUIT MINISTRY
Chicago

LOYOLA PRESS.
A JESUIT MINISTRY

3441 N. Ashland Avenue
Chicago, Illinois 60657
(800) 621-1008
www.loyolapress.com

Scripture quotations contained herein are from the New Revised Standard
Version Bible: Catholic Edition, copyright © 1993 and 1989 by the Division of
Christian Education of the National Council of the Churches of Christ in the
U.S.A. Used by permission. All rights reserved.

Cover image The Crosiers/Gene Plaisted, OSC.

Library of Congress Cataloging-in-Publication Data
Harrington, Daniel J.
  Meeting St. Mark today / Daniel J. Harrington.
    p. cm.
  ISBN-13: 978-0-8294-2915-2
  ISBN-10: 0-8294-2915-8
1. Bible. N.T. Mark--Commentaries. 2. Suffering--Biblical teaching. I. Title.
II. Title: Meeting Saint Mark today.
  BS2585.53.H36 2011
  226.3'07--dc23
                                                      2011022294

Printed in the United States of America
11 12 13 14 15 Versa 10 9 8 7 6 5 4 3 2 1

Contents

Part Three: The Gospel of Suffering in Context

Part Four: Mark's Gospel in Christian Life

A Year Dedicated to St. Mark: The Gospel of Suffering

Mark's Gospel is now generally regarded as the earliest Gospel. It presents a stark and challenging portrait of Jesus' public ministry, which leads into a dramatic account of his passion and death. It has often been described as a passion narrative with a long introduction. Mark presents Jesus as a wise teacher and a powerful and compassionate healer. But he also insists that this Jesus can be properly understood only when we confront the mystery of the cross and Jesus' identity as a suffering Messiah. For this reason Mark's work is sometimes called the Gospel of Suffering. As we study and pray through this text, we will have to face the suffering of Jesus the Son of God and the suffering that is part of our lives as individuals and as citizens of the world.

In the Year B (2012, 2015, 2018, 2021, 2024, etc.) in the Catholic Church's lectionary of Scripture readings for Mass, the Gospel passage almost every Sunday is taken from St. Mark's Gospel. In the New Testament we meet St. Mark mainly through the Gospel that bears his name. Throughout the centuries and especially in the church's lectionary before Vatican II, Mark's Gospel was badly neglected. For much of Christian history (due largely to the influence of St. Augustine), Mark was considered a poor imitation of Matthew and Luke. However, in the nineteenth century, biblical scholars began to recognize that in fact Matthew and Luke were revised and expanded versions of Mark, and that Mark's Gospel had been composed earlier than the other two. In the twentieth century, biblical scholars and literary critics came to appreciate better the artistry of Mark's Gospel and the literary skill of the Evangelist behind it. In recent years, Mark's Gospel has become the testing ground for applying new literary, historical, and social-scientific methods to biblical and other ancient texts.

After an introduction to what we know with some certainty about the author of Mark's Gospel and its major theological themes, this book provides

- Chapters 2–7: a *narrative analysis* of the entire Gospel. These chapters focus on the Gospel's key words and images, characters, plot, literary forms, indications of time and place, and theological message.
- Chapters 8–9: a focus first on how Mark portrays the suffering of Jesus and then on the various approaches to suffering found throughout the Bible.
- Chapter 10: reflections on the biblical theme of suffering in which Mark is the lead text.
- Questions for reflection and discussion are provided in each chapter, and this book can be used easily by Bible study groups.

For a much fuller treatment of Mark's Gospel and related topics, I suggest consulting the major commentary by John R. Donahue and myself entitled *The Gospel of Mark* in the Sacra Pagina series published by the Liturgical Press (2002), and reprinted in a paperback edition with an updated bibliography (2005). I am grateful to Loyola Press for the invitation to synthesize my views on Mark's Gospel and to present them to a wider audience.

PART ONE

Meeting St. Mark

In those days Jesus came from Nazareth of Galilee and was baptized by John in the Jordan. And just as he was coming up out of the water, he saw the heavens torn apart and the spirit descending like a dove on him. And a voice came from heaven, "You are my Son, the Beloved; with you I am well pleased."

—Mark 1:9–11

1

The Evangelist and His Gospel

What we call the Gospel of Mark is technically an anonymous composition—as are the other Gospels. The Evangelist never identifies himself by name or claims to have been a participant in or an eyewitness to the events he describes. The traditional title "According to Mark" seems not to have been part of the original text but rather a later addition made in keeping with the early church's custom of attributing this Gospel to "Mark."

But who was this Mark? In the early Christian tradition someone named Mark has close ties to both Paul and Peter. The Pauline epistles mention a person named Mark (a common name in the Greco-Roman world) three different times. There is a reference to Mark in the list of Paul's coworkers in Philemon 24. Colossians 4:10 refers to "Mark the cousin of Barnabas." And in 2 Timothy 4:11 Paul urges Timothy to "get Mark and bring him with you, for he is useful in my ministry."

In the Acts of the Apostles there are three more mentions of someone named Mark. According to Acts 12:12, the "house of Mary, the mother of John whose other name was Mark" was a center for the early Christian community in Jerusalem. According to Acts 12:25, "John, whose other name was Mark" returned to Jerusalem with Paul and Barnabas after completing their apostolic mission in Antioch. And Acts 15:37–39 describes a disagreement between Paul and Barnabas over "John called Mark." Paul refused to take John Mark along on their next apostolic mission because he "had deserted them in Pamphylia and had not accompanied them in the work" (15:38). The result was that Barnabas and Mark went off to Cyprus, and Paul and Silas went through Syria and Cilicia.

In 1 Peter 5:13 there is another reference to someone named Mark: "Your sister church in Babylon . . . sends you greetings; and so does my son Mark." Bible scholars generally acknowledge that here (and in Revelation), "Babylon" is a code name for Rome. Thus, 1 Peter 5:13 links Mark with Peter and Rome. The earliest evidence from the church regarding the authorship of this Gospel comes from "the Elder" as quoted by Papias (in the early second century) as quoted by Eusebius (in his *Ecclesiastical History* 3.39.15): "Mark, having become the interpreter of Peter, wrote down accurately whatever he remembered of what was said or done by the Lord, but not in order." While this statement raises many questions, it does connect Mark and his Gospel to Peter and Rome. This tradition is repeated by many other writers of the early church.

The identity of Mark and the authorship of the Gospel that now bears his name are complicated issues. For our purposes the name "Mark" will be used to refer to the early Christian writer who put this Gospel into its final form (that is, something much like what has come down to us in the Christian Bible). It is through the Gospel of Mark that we can best meet St. Mark today. Keep in mind that this book is not a biography of Mark; it is an examination of Mark's "biography" of Jesus.

Christians in Rome

The oldest and best tradition relates Mark's Gospel to the Roman Christian community that suffered persecution in the wake of Emperor Nero's efforts to blame the Christians for the great fire of A.D. 64. The material in Mark's Gospel fits well with the tradition presented by the Roman historian Tacitus in *Annales* 15.44. Tacitus describes the procedure used in arresting the Christians at that time: "First, then, the confessed members of the sect were arrested; next, on evidence furnished by them a huge multitude was convicted not so much on the count of arson as hatred of the human race." Tacitus goes on to recount the horrible punishments inflicted on them: "They were covered with wild beasts' skins and torn to death by dogs; or they were fastened on crosses, and when daylight failed were burned to serve as lamps by night."

In my view, the original audience for Mark's Gospel was the Roman Christian community made up of both Jewish and Gentile Christians. By this time (around A.D. 70), it was very likely that most of the Christians in Rome were Gentiles. So, the Evangelist feels obliged to explain certain Jewish customs and practices, most famously in 7:3–4 about washing cups and dishes as well as hands. But the Evangelist himself seems to have been a Jew. Though he makes some mistakes about Scripture texts and concludes that Jesus declared all foods clean in Mark 7:19 (a point Matthew "corrected" by omitting it in Matthew 15), he knows a good deal about Judaism and is committed to presenting Jesus within the context of first-century Palestinian Judaism. The traditions that relate Mark to Peter and to Paul also appear to assume that Mark was a Jew. And so I read Mark as a Gospel written by a Jewish Christian author about Jesus the Jew, for a mixed Jewish and Gentile Christian audience in Rome around A.D. 70.

However, a recent trend among some biblical scholars is to place the composition of Mark's Gospel in the eastern part of the Mediterranean world (in Syria or Galilee), and to relate it to events connected with the Jewish Revolt in Palestine and the destruction of the Jerusalem temple in A.D. 70. I still prefer the Roman tradition. In either case (Rome or Syria-Palestine), Mark's Gospel seems to have circulated rather quickly around the Mediterranean world, and it was revised and expanded independently by the Evangelists we know as Matthew and Luke some ten to fifteen years later. Both writers included far more teaching material than Mark did, from sources not available to Mark.

Given this history, it appears that Mark's Gospel is the oldest complete Gospel in the Christian Scriptures, and that in a real sense Mark invented the literary genre we call Gospel—that is, a connected narrative about Jesus of Nazareth that describes his activities and his teachings in Galilee and Judea, as well as his passion, death, and resurrection in Jerusalem around A.D. 30. Mark had access to various written and oral traditions about Jesus (controversies, parables, aphorisms, miracle stories, and so forth) that had circulated in early Christian communities for some forty years. Thus, Mark was very much a transmitter and arranger of traditional materials.

At the same time, Mark was an interpreter of traditions and an author in his own right. As the narrative analysis that follows will show, Mark put his distinctive stylistic stamp on the material. For example, he liked the word *immediately*, used double time expressions, included vivid details, and changed scenes rapidly. He frequently employed the literary technique in which he begins one story, interrupts it with another story, and returns to the first story. The effect is that the two narratives interpret one another. This device, known to scholars as intercalation, is sometimes called Mark's "sandwich" technique.

In presenting his story of Jesus, Mark followed a geographical outline. In the first half of the Gospel he describes Jesus' activities and teachings in Galilee and the areas surrounding it. Next there is a journey from northern Galilee to Jerusalem. Then Jesus arrives in Jerusalem, exercises a brief teaching ministry, and there he is arrested, executed, and is raised from the dead. The result is what looks like a biography of Jesus, at least with regard to his public ministry and his passion and death.

Mark wrote his Gospel in order to inform and encourage followers of Jesus. After some forty years of missionary activity, the time was ripe for someone to bring together the various traditions about Jesus and situate them in the context of Jesus' public ministry. Not only that, the Christians for whom Mark originally wrote were undergoing persecution, or at least the threat of persecution. They needed Jesus' own good example of fidelity to bolster their spirits and help them stay faithful to their beliefs.

Also, Mark sought to shed light on some difficult questions that all early Christians had to face. How could Jesus be the Son of God if he had died a criminal's death, crucified on the Roman instrument of execution—what we now refer to simply as "the cross"? If he really was the Messiah of Jewish expectations, why did he not claim it openly and do what the Messiah was expected to do? What was the relationship between Jesus' teachings and Jewish speculations about the end of the world? And what was the relationship between Jesus' followers and members of other Jewish religious movements?

Mark's Gospel presents Jesus as fulfilling the hopes of God's people expressed in the Old Testament and carrying on his ministry in the land of Israel around A.D. 30. Mark tells Jesus' story in terms of names and titles intelligible only within Judaism, in the framework of Jewish beliefs about the end-times, and in conflict with other Jewish movements and the temple establishment but in sympathy with certain other Jews.

Mark's Use of the Old Testament

At many pivotal points in his story of Jesus, Mark appeals to Old Testament texts and appears to assume that his readers know these texts and regard them as authoritative. That Mark respected the Jewish Scriptures is clear from Mark 1:2–3, where he uses a quotation from "the prophet Isaiah" to explain the relationship between John the Baptist ("the voice") and Jesus ("the Lord"). His failure to note that the first part of this quotation came not from Isaiah but from Exodus 23:20 and Malachi 3:1

suggests that here Mark may have had access to a collection of biblical proof texts, or *testimonia*, or at least that he was not as conversant with the Old Testament as Matthew was. Matthew used only the Isaiah part in Matthew 3:3 and shifted the Exodus 23:20/Malachi 3:1 part to Matthew 11:10. Another mistake in Mark's use of the Old Testament occurs at 2:26, where he says that Abiathar (rather than Ahimelech) was the priest when David demanded the bread of the presence (see 1 Samuel 21:1–6).

There are an impressive number of explicit Old Testament quotations in Mark's account of Jesus' public ministry, especially from Isaiah, Psalms, and Daniel. Jesus appeals to Isaiah 6:9–10 ("they may indeed look, but not perceive") to explain why outsiders (4:12) and even his own disciples (8:18) fail to understand his preaching about God's kingdom. In his critique of the Pharisees' traditions about ritual defilement (7:6–7), Jesus quotes Isaiah 29:13: "Because these people draw near with their mouths and honor me with their lips, while their hearts are far from me, and their worship of me is a human commandment learned by rote." The crowd's acclamation of Jesus in 7:37 ("He has done everything well; he even makes the deaf to hear and the mute to speak") is an echo of Isaiah 35:5–6.

In Mark 11:9–10, when Jesus enters Jerusalem, he is greeted with words from Psalm 118:26: "Blessed is the one who comes in the name of the Lord." In Mark 11:17, his symbolic action in "cleansing" the temple is justified by an appeal to the combination of Isaiah 56:7 and Jeremiah 7:11: "My house shall be called a house of prayer for all the nations. But you have made it a den of robbers." His parable of the wicked tenants (12:1–12) ends with a quotation of Psalm 118:22–23: "The stone that the builders rejected has become the chief cornerstone." In 12:35–37 he presents an interpretation of Psalm 110:1 ("the LORD says to my Lord") designed to show the superiority of the title "Lord" to "Messiah" and "Son of David." When Jesus speaks of end-times in Mark 13, many of the major terms and concepts—the great tribulation, the abomination of desolation, the glorious Son of Man, and the resurrection of the dead—come from the book of Daniel.

One of the great themes of Mark's passion narrative is expressed by Jesus in 14:49: "Let the scriptures be fulfilled." On the Mount of Olives (14:27), Jesus quotes Zechariah 13:7 ("I will strike the shepherd, and the sheep will be scattered") as a prophecy that his disciples would soon desert him. At his trial before the Sanhedrin (14:62), Jesus identifies himself as the glorious Son of Man with words taken from Daniel 7:13. And in chapter 15 there are enough quotations and allusions to Isaiah 53 and Psalm 22 to describe Jesus as the personification of the Suffering Servant and the Suffering Righteous One (see also Wisdom 2:12–20).

Mark's Theological Geography

Mark's Gospel is a story mainly about Jesus of Nazareth. It is set in the land of Israel and follows a theological-geographical outline.

- Galilee functions as the place where Jesus' authority is revealed.
- The journey from Galilee to Judea is the occasion for Jesus to teach about his identity and discipleship.
- Jerusalem is the place of his rejection and death.

The prologue: 1:1–13

Mark tells the reader that John the Baptist prepared the way for Jesus (thus fulfilling Old Testament prophecies), that a voice from heaven declared Jesus to be "my Son, the Beloved," and that Jesus withstood testing by Satan. The prologue has the effect of identifying Jesus as the Son of God and placing him and his public ministry in a cosmic battle with Satan.

First major section: 1:14—8:21

Mark describes how Jesus the anointed Son of God proclaims in the Galilee region the imminence of God's reign through his teachings and actions. At the same time, Mark shows that Jesus encounters misunderstanding and opposition from many groups. The scene of Jesus' activity is Galilee and the surrounding area, which in Mark's theological geography is the place for the revelation or manifestation of Jesus as a powerful teacher and healer. The summary statement places everything that Jesus says and does in the context of his proclamation of God's kingdom: "The time is fulfilled, and the kingdom of God has come near" (1:15).

Second major section: 8:22—10:52

This part of the story concerns the journey from Galilee to Jerusalem. Mark introduces and concludes this section with stories in which blind men come to see. Throughout the journey from Caesarea Philippi in northern Galilee to Jerusalem, the Jesus of Mark's Gospel instructs his disciples (and Mark's readers) about his identity as the Son of Man who must suffer, die, and rise from the dead, and about what it means to follow him.

Third major section: 11:1—16:8

Jerusalem is the primary place in which Jesus is rejected. After his provocative symbolic actions in entering the city and cleansing the temple, Jesus debates various Jewish groups. When asked about the destruction of the Jerusalem temple, Jesus takes the conversation to the cosmic level and looks forward to the coming of the Son of Man in glory as the sign of the fullness of God's kingdom.

In the events leading up to Jesus' arrest, he remains very much in command (even though the Gethsemane episode shows that he struggles to accept death on the cross as his Father's will), in that he knows what is going to happen and is confident that the Scriptures are being fulfilled. In the trials before the Sanhedrin and Pilate, Jesus appears as Messiah/Son of God and as the Suffering Servant of Isaiah 53.

In the crucifixion story, Jesus is the embodiment of Psalm 22, the psalm of the suffering righteous person. The confession by the Roman centurion at the moment of Jesus' death ("Truly this man was God's Son!") is the first recognition by a human in Mark's Gospel (and by a Gentile no less!) about Jesus' real identity—something that Mark's readers have known since the beginning of the story.

The women disciples, who are introduced only at 15:40–41, witness the death of Jesus and his burial. And they discover his tomb to be empty on Easter Sunday morning. The explanation offered by the young man at the tomb is that "he has been raised." Jesus, the suffering Son of Man, who personifies the Suffering Righteous One of Psalm 22 and the Suffering Servant of Isaiah 53, has been vindicated in his resurrection from the dead.

Names and Titles of Jesus

The major titles that Mark applies to Jesus—Son of God, Messiah, and Son of Man—were already traditional among early Christians when Mark wrote his Gospel. Nevertheless, if the first readers were to understand these titles properly, they needed to be familiar with Judaism and the Old Testament. Mark used the titles to situate Jesus in a Jewish environment.

Son of God

In the Old Testament the title "Son of God" is applied to

- Israel as God's people (Hosea 11:1)
- the king at his coronation (Psalm 2:7)
- the angels (Job 38:7)
- and the suffering righteous person (Wisdom 2:18).

In Mark's Gospel, "Son of God" is a very prominent title for Jesus.

- 1:1 (in most manuscripts). "The beginning of the good news of Jesus Christ, the Son of God."
- 1:11. At Jesus' baptism a voice from heaven proclaims: "You are my Son, the Beloved."
- 3:11. Demons, or "unclean spirits," recognize Jesus as "the Son of God."
- 5:7. Demons recognize Jesus as the "Son of the Most High God."
- 9:7. At Jesus' transfiguration a voice from heaven proclaims, "This is my Son, the Beloved."

- 12:1–12. In the parable of the vineyard, it is hard to escape the implication that the son is Jesus ("a beloved son . . . my son").
- 13:32. In claiming that only the Father knows "that day or hour," Jesus seems to refer to himself as the Son of God.
- 14:61–62. When at the Sanhedrin trial the chief priest asks whether Jesus is "the Son of the Blessed One," Jesus answers, "I am."
- 15:39. Finally at the moment of Jesus' death on the cross, the Roman centurion proclaims, "Truly this man was God's Son!" In Mark's narrative, the first time a human (who happens to be a Gentile) recognizes Jesus' true identity as the Son of God is at the time of his death!

Messiah/Anointed one

The Hebrew word for "anointed one" is *mashiah*. The Greek translation is *christos*. Priests, prophets, and kings in Judaism's early history (the Old Testament) were anointed to signify that God had chosen them for specific roles and services. In New Testament times there was no single Jewish concept of Messiah, and much depends on the context in which the term appears. Mark employs the Greek word *christos* ("anointed") for the Hebrew *mashiah*.

- 1:1. Mark uses "Christ" as a surname for Jesus ("the good news of Jesus Christ"), a practice that was common by the time the letters of Paul were written.
- 9:41. Jesus speaks about one who bears "the name of Christ."

- 12:35–37. Jesus relates "Messiah" and "son of David."
- 13:21. Jesus warns about those who might say, "Look! Here is the Messiah."

The most distinctive and theologically important occurrences of *christos* in Mark's Gospel appear during Jesus' suffering and death.

- 8:29, 31. When Peter confesses that Jesus is the Messiah/ Christ, almost immediately Jesus utters his first passion prediction that "the Son of Man must undergo great suffering."
- 14:61–62. At the trial before the Sanhedrin, the high priest asks Jesus, "Are you the Messiah/Christ . . . ?" and Jesus answers, "I am."
- 15:32. And as Jesus is lifted up on the cross, the chief priests and scribes taunt him: "Let the Messiah/Christ, the King of Israel, come down."

The appearance of the title "Messiah/Christ" in the context of Jesus' suffering and death—in some of the most significant passages in the Gospel—suggests that Mark is deliberately redefining the title with reference to Jesus. Mark's point seems to be that Jesus' messiahship involves suffering, and that Jesus cannot be understood as the Messiah/Christ apart from the mystery of the cross.

Two variants of Messiah/Christ are "Son of David" and "King of the Jews." The former title is used twice by Bartimaeus in 10:47–48: "Son of David, have mercy on me!" The name "Son of David" also appears in the controversy about the interpretation of Psalm 110:1, when Jesus asks, in 12:35, "How can the scribes say that the Messiah/Christ is the Son of David?" The "King of the Jews" is the "outsider" Roman translation of "Messiah/Christ," and it occurs exclusively in chapter 15 (verses 2, 9, 12, 18, 26).

In Mark's Gospel, Jesus keeps his identity hidden until the proper time, an aspect of the story scholars have referred to as the "messianic secret." The clearest and most important example of this comes immediately after Peter's confession of Jesus as the Messiah/Christ. There Mark adds in 8:30: "And he sternly ordered them not to tell anyone about him." This is the only case in which there is a direct connection between the title of "Messiah" being applied to Jesus and his commanding the disciples to keep quiet about it. The passages that are often lumped together in the category of the "messianic secret" involve instances that are connected loosely, if at all: Jesus' instructions for people to remain silent after he had performed miracles (1:25, 34, 44; 3:12; 5:43; 7:36); Jesus' private instructions for his disciples (4:11, 34; 7:17; 9:28, 31–50; 13:3–36); and his unsuccessful efforts at hiding from the public (6:31; 7:24; 9:30). The best explanation for this phenomenon is that Mark sought to redefine the term "Messiah" and other titles in the light of Jesus' death and resurrection, and so he put off revealing Jesus' true identity until his death (see 15:39) and his resurrection (see 9:9).

Son of Man

In the Old Testament the prophet Ezekiel is frequently addressed by God as "son of man" (*ben adam* in Hebrew) and told to prophesy (see 2:1, 3, 6, 8; 3:1, 3, etc.). In Daniel 7:13 a figure described as "one like a son of man" (*bar enash* in Aramaic) receives from the

"Ancient of Days" dominion and glory and kingship. In *1 Enoch* 48, the "Son of Man" is a preexistent heavenly being who passes judgment upon all human and angelic beings.

In Mark's Gospel "Son of Man" is a prominent title for Jesus.

The most distinctive and theologically important uses of "Son of Man" (*ho hyios tou anthropou)* appear during Jesus' passion, death, and resurrection. This title is part of the three passion predictions (8:31; 9:31; 10:33–34). It occurs two more times in the conversation about Jesus' death and resurrection after the Transfiguration (9:9, 12). It also appears in the pivotal declaration of Jesus toward the end of the journey from Galilee to Jerusalem: "For the Son of Man came . . . to give his life as a ransom for many" (10:45).

A second category of "Son of Man" sayings in Mark is like the "son of man" in Ezekiel. In several places Jesus uses "Son of Man" to refer to himself and his authority to forgive sins (2:10) and in his role as Lord of the Sabbath (2:28). At the Last Supper Jesus remarks that "the Son of Man goes as it is written of him" (14:21), and at his arrest he observes that "the Son of Man is betrayed into the hands of sinners" (14:41). In all these cases one gets the sense that more is meant than "I." There is a solemnity to these sayings and a suggestion that Jesus is a very significant "son of man/Adam."

The third category of Mark's "Son of Man" sayings is more in line with Daniel 7 and *1 Enoch* 48. In 8:38 Jesus warns that the

Son of Man will be ashamed of people who are ashamed of him and his words, "when he comes in the glory of his Father with the holy angels." The apocalyptic scenario developed in Mark 13 reaches its climax in 13:26 with the vision of "the Son of Man coming in the clouds," which is a clear allusion to Daniel 7:13. At the trial before the Sanhedrin, Jesus again alludes to Daniel 7:13 when he promises, "you will see the Son of Man seated at the right hand of the Power, and coming with the clouds of heaven" (14:62). In all three cases there can be little doubt that Mark identifies the glorious end-times Son of Man as Jesus.

Other titles

In the Gospel of Mark, John the Baptist's preaching about "one who is more powerful" (1:7) also functions as a title for Jesus. In 1:24 the demon being exorcised correctly identifies Jesus as "the Holy One of God."

Mark does not do much with "prophet" as a title for Jesus, especially when compared to Luke-Acts. While Jesus explains his rejection at Nazareth as being due to his identity as a prophet ("prophets are not without honor" 6:4), elsewhere the title is reserved for Isaiah (1:2) and John the Baptist (11:32) or is cited as one of the popular but inadequate perceptions of Jesus (6:15; 8:28).

Likewise, "Lord" (*Kyrios*) is not as prominent a title for Jesus in Mark's Gospel as it is in Matthew's. The term is generally used as a title for God, the Father of Jesus (see 11:9; 12:11; 12:29–30; 12:36–37; 13:20) as it is used in the Greek Old Testament. In 5:19 and 11:3 Jesus uses *Kyrios* to refer to himself, and there it may not have much theological significance but may refer to Jesus' role of teacher or "master." In 1:3 ("Prepare the way of the Lord"), its occurrence in Isaiah 40:3 is assumed to refer to Jesus. In the debate about interpreting Psalm 110:1 ("The LORD said to my Lord"), the second "Lord" is taken to imply the superiority of this title to "Messiah/Christ" and "Son of David."

Last Things

The images and concepts of Jewish apocalyptic or end-times beliefs ("the last things") permeate Mark's Gospel—so much so that it has been aptly called an apocalyptic drama. The Evangelist's summary of Jesus' preaching appears in Mark 1:15: "The time is fulfilled, and the kingdom of God has come near; repent, and believe in the good news." This summary situates Mark's story of Jesus in the context of end times. The main topic is the kingdom of God—that moment when all creation will acknowledge the sovereignty of God and proceed according to God's original plan. While the kingdom's fullness is future, the teaching and healing activity of Jesus represent its present reality dramatically. Jesus' proclamation of the future and present dimensions of God's kingdom demands an appropriate response: conversion, and faith in the good news that Jesus brings.

The testing of Jesus by Satan (1:12–13) alerts the reader to Mark's idea that Jesus' ministry is a struggle against the cosmic forces of evil. Mark's story assumes dual (but not equal) forces in the world, a concept found in the Dead Sea scrolls (the Prince of Light with the children of light versus the Prince of Darkness with the children of darkness; see the Qumran *Rule of the Community*

3—4). Jesus' first public activities—his exorcisms, healings, and debates with hostile opponents—are decisive moments in the struggle against the forces of the Evil One. The debate with the scribes in 3:20–30 makes it clear that the origin of Jesus' power as a teacher and healer is the Holy Spirit, and that he stands against the one who is called Satan/Beelzebul/Prince of Demons.

The parables in 4:1–34 impart some basic teachings about the kingdom of God. God brings about the kingdom; there is a contrast between its small beginnings in the present and its future fullness; something decisive is happening in Jesus' ministry; and Jesus' proclamation of God's kingdom deserves an enthusiastic and fruitful response. The power of Jesus as the herald of God's kingdom is illustrated by his deeds in 4:35—5:43. He shows himself to be the master of those forces that in Jewish and ancient Near Eastern traditions appear to be under the dominion of Satan: the storm at sea, the demons, sickness and the suffering it brings, and death.

Having placed Jesus' ministry in the context of a cosmic struggle against the forces of evil, Mark (from chapter 6 onward) pits Jesus against misunderstanding and hostility from human opponents: the people of Nazareth, his own disciples, and the chief priests, elders, and scribes of Jerusalem. In the midst of this story we are given the Transfiguration account, which provides insight into, and an anticipation of, the true nature of Jesus as the glorious Son of Man. And in Jesus' discussion of the end-times, he describes the climactic event: "Then they will see 'the Son of Man coming in clouds' with great power and glory" (13:26). Since these events are to take place in "this generation" (13:30)—though the precise time remains unknown (see 13:32)—the appropriate religious and ethical response is constant vigilance (13:33–37).

In Jewish theology of Jesus' time, resurrection was understood to be an event that happened at the end of earthly time (see Daniel 12:1–3). In Mark 12:18–27 Jesus stands with the Pharisees against the Sadducees, and argues that resurrection is in the Torah (Exodus 3:6, 15–16) and within the power of God. In Mark's narrative Jesus is the first case of resurrection. According to 16:6, the reason Jesus' tomb was found empty was that "he has been raised." In the resurrection of Jesus a decisive event of the end-times he predicted has already taken place in "this generation."

Jesus and the Jews

Scholars often cite Mark's comment about Jewish traditions regarding ritual purity in 7:3–4 as evidence that Mark wrote for a predominantly non-Jewish audience. This may be so. But if Mark expected his first readers to understand most of his story of Jesus, he had to assume that they knew a good deal about "things Jewish" and were interested in them. He tells the story of Jesus as a Jewish teacher and healer, who gathered Jewish disciples, worked in Galilee and Judea, and died with the words of Psalm 22:1 on his lips ("My God, my God, why have you forsaken me?"). Jesus' debates with various Jewish groups deal almost entirely with Jewish topics, and his positions on these matters are generally within the range of opinions represented by other first-century Jewish teachers.

While Mark's Jesus is clearly Jewish, Mark also presents his hero as superior to other Jewish teachers and healers and as possessing significance for non-Jews as well (see 7:24—8:10). During his Galilean ministry Jesus engages fellow Jews in debate, and his initial success results in a plot against him by Pharisees and Herodians. During his ministry in Jerusalem, Jesus has more controversies with various Jewish groups and gains the envy and hostility of the chief priests, elders, and scribes there. While these Jewish officials take the initiative in having Jesus arrested and condemned to death, it is the Roman prefect Pontius Pilate who is ultimately responsible for Jesus' execution.

From his entry into Jerusalem at the beginning of Mark 11, Jesus is critical of the Jerusalem temple and those who are responsible for it. His action in the temple complex is sandwiched between sections about the withered fig tree. Jesus' temple action and his prophecy about the destruction of the temple are major issues in his later trial before the Sanhedrin and at his crucifixion. And those who plot Jesus' arrest and execution (most obviously the chief priests) stand to lose the most if Jesus' prophecies about the temple come to pass.

So Mark's Jesus has conflicts with other Jews and Jewish groups. But these facts hardly set Jesus outside the boundaries of Judaism in the first century. As the Dead Sea scrolls have shown abundantly, Judaism in Jesus' time was both diverse and contentious, and there was strong opposition to the Jerusalem temple and its officials from Jews other than Jesus.

A little-noticed feature in Mark's narrative of Jesus is the presence of Jewish characters who do not belong to the Jesus movement and yet act in ways that are regarded as exemplary or praiseworthy. One such figure is the exorcist who casts out demons in Jesus' name, but who does not follow Jesus as a disciple (Mark 9:38). When told of this, Jesus takes a tolerant attitude and says: "Whoever is not against us is for us" (9:40). The episode occurs while Jesus and his disciples are still in Galilee, and it appears that the Evangelist wants us to assume that the strange exorcist is a Jew. At least nothing suggests that he is a Gentile.

Later, a man confronts Jesus and asks him: "What must I do to inherit eternal life?" Jesus instructs him to keep the commandments and lists examples taken mainly from the Ten Commandments: "You shall not murder; You shall not commit adultery; . . ." We are then told that Jesus had great personal affection for the questioner: "Jesus, looking at him, loved him." Jesus goes on to challenge the man to sell his possessions and to follow Jesus as his disciple. The man, who is rich, rejects the invitation and goes away "grieving." His attachment to his material possessions then becomes the occasion for various teachings about possessions as an obstacle to entering the kingdom of God. What gets overlooked in Mark 10:17–22 is Jesus' initial response to the effect that the rich man—surely a Jew in this context—can inherit eternal life by keeping the commandments in the Torah.

The debate about the "great commandment" in Mark 12:28–34 is not so much a controversy or conflict as it is a pleasant conversation between Jesus and a scribe. When the scribe asks, "Which commandment is the first of all?" Jesus responds by quoting Deuteronomy 6:4–5 (love God) and Leviticus 19:18 (love your neighbor). The scribe expresses enthusiastic agreement with Jesus ("You are right, Teacher"), and declares that observing the two love commandments is more important than all holocausts and sacrifices. Jesus in turn approves the wisdom of the scribe's answer and states: "You are not far from the kingdom of God." One gets the impression that in some contexts, such as this exchange and the one with the rich young man in Mark 10, the term "kingdom of God" is tied to Jesus and his movement but following Jesus does not exhaust the possibilities of inheriting eternal life. At any rate, in Mark 12, a Jewish scribe expresses enthusiastic approval of Jesus' teaching (which is, of course, an affirmation of the Torah), and is given high praise in return.

The person responsible for the burial of Jesus, according to Mark 15:43–46, is Joseph of Arimathea, surely a Jew. In Mark's narrative it is not clear that Joseph was a disciple of Jesus, even though Matthew 27:57 and John 19:38 clearly identify him as one. Indeed, according to Mark's narrative, as a "respected member of the council," Joseph seems to have been a member of the Jewish Sanhedrin that sentenced Jesus to death: "All of them condemned him as deserving death" (14:64). Also, it is unlikely that the Roman prefect Pontius Pilate would have entrusted Jesus' corpse to someone known to be a member of his movement. The way in which Mark describes Joseph of Arimathea and his actions after Jesus' death might be explained as coming from Joseph's desire to give Jesus a decent burial before the Sabbath (in accord with Deuteronomy 21:22–23). What inspires Joseph is not so much his personal relationship to Jesus, whom he barely knows, but rather his devotion to fulfilling the biblical commandment to bury a fellow Jew on the day of his death.

His action is reminiscent of Tobit's zeal to bury his fellow Jews in the Diaspora (see Tobit 1:17–18; 2:3–4, 7–8). Mark may portray Joseph of Arimathea as simply a righteous Jew outside the circle of Jesus. Throughout Mark's Gospel, Jesus relates with other Jews, both positively and negatively.

For Reflection and Discussion

What do you hope to gain as you begin your journey with Jesus according to Mark?

Which title of Jesus is most meaningful to you right now?

Is there suffering in your life now? Do you relate it to Jesus' suffering?

PART TWO

Mark's Story of Jesus

As soon as they left the synagogue, they entered the house of Simon and Andrew, with James and John. Now Simon's mother-in-law was in bed with a fever, and they told him about her at once. He came and took her by the hand and lifted her up. Then the fever left her, and she began to serve them.

That evening, at sunset, they brought to him all who were sick or possessed with demons. And the whole city was gathered around the door. And he cured many who were sick with various diseases, and cast out many demons; and he would not permit the demons to speak, because they knew him.

—Mark 1:29–34

2

Jesus' Authority Is Revealed in Galilee

Mark 1:1—3:6

The prologue in Mark 1:1–13 provides the readers with important information about Jesus that the characters (apart from Jesus) in the story that follows do not have. In the title (1:1), Jesus is identified as the "Christ" (the Messiah of Israel's hopes) and as the "Son of God." What kind of Son of God he is will be revealed, especially at the trial before the Jewish officials and at the cross (for the centurion's confession of him, see 15:39). The "good news" refers to the saving significance of Jesus' life, death, and resurrection. Mark has chosen to present this good news in the form of a story about Jesus' public career and his passion and death, thus establishing the Christian literary genre we know as the "Gospel."

Introducing Jesus

1:1–11. Mark's story of Jesus begins with John the Baptist. According to Mark, the task of John the Baptist was to prepare

the way for Jesus. This is made clear first of all in 1:2–3 by a combination of Old Testament quotations (Exodus 23:20; Isaiah 40:3;
Malachi 3:1) attributed to Isaiah. In 1:4–6 Mark describes in turn
John's baptism ("repentance for the forgiveness of sins"), the popular enthusiasm he generated, and his ascetic and prophetic lifestyle
after the pattern of Elijah (2 Kings 1:8). However, according to
John's own words in 1:7–8, all his activity was preparation for the
appearance of Jesus as the "more powerful" one, whose baptism
with the Holy Spirit will far surpass John's baptism with water.

The four Gospels agree that Jesus was associated with John's
movement and underwent John's baptism. Nevertheless, even as
Jesus accepts John's baptism, Mark emphasizes Jesus' superiority
to John in 1:9–11. What is most important in Mark's account is
the identity of Jesus that is announced at the baptism: "You are my
Son, the Beloved; with you I am well pleased." The announcement
is preceded by three biblical symbols of divine communication:
the heavens torn apart (Isaiah 64:1), the Spirit's dovelike descent
(Genesis 1:2), and the voice from heaven. The voice's proclamation identifies Jesus as the Son of God (Psalm 2:7), God's Beloved
(Genesis 22:2, 12, 16), and God's Servant (Isaiah 42:1–2).

**1:12–13. What kind of Son of God Jesus is becomes clear
in Mark's brief account of the testing, or "temptation," of
Jesus (compare Matthew 4:1–11 and Luke 4:1–13).** In the
Bible, the wilderness can be both a place of danger and a place
where one encounters God. Jesus' forty days of fasting recalls
the similar fasts undertaken by Moses (Deuteronomy 9:18) and
Elijah (1 Kings 19:8), as well as ancient Israel's forty years of testing in the wilderness after their escape from slavery in Egypt. Led

by the Spirit, Jesus overcomes the tests imposed on him by Satan and shows himself to be the faithful Son of God. His apparently peaceful coexistence with the wild beasts, and the angelic ministrations to him point forward to the new creation that Jesus' death and resurrection will bring about.

1:14–15. Mark's summary of the good news that Jesus embodies, proclaims, and enacts provides a transition or bridge between the prologue and the body of the Gospel. He leaves John in the past (though his arrest and execution will be described in detail by the flashback in 6:14–29), and situates Jesus' initial public activity in his home area of Galilee. The focus of Jesus' preaching and miracle working will be the kingdom of God. His ministry comes at the right time; in him God's kingdom has indeed drawn near—that is, Jesus inaugurates a new phase of history that moves humanity toward the future fullness of God's kingdom. The proper response to what Jesus reveals involves changing one's life ("repent") and believing in the "good news" that Jesus proclaims in his preaching and represents through his powerful actions.

1:16–20. Jesus' call of his first disciples takes place by the Sea of Galilee and involves two sets of brothers—Simon (Peter) and Andrew, and James and John—who happen to be fishermen. When Jesus summons them to "Follow me," these men respond immediately and leave behind their businesses and families. Mark mentions no prior contact with Jesus, which serves only to highlight his personal attractiveness and persuasiveness. The story shows that from the beginning Jesus involves other people in his mission, and it becomes the model for other "call" stories in Mark's

Gospel (see 2:13–14; 3:13–19; 6:6b–13). According to Mark, the essence of discipleship is being with Jesus and sharing in his mission. The first followers of Jesus will continue to be fishermen, but now they will be "fishing" for people (see Jeremiah 16:16).

Jesus' Typical Day

Capernaum, a fishing village on the western shore of the Sea of Galilee, becomes the site for the beginning of Jesus' public activity as a teacher and a healer. The three episodes in 1:21–34 are presented as a "typical day" in Jesus' early ministry. The day is identified as a Sabbath (1:21).

1:21–28. The first episode takes place in the synagogue, the gathering place for Jews in the area. By his authoritative teaching Jesus astounds the congregation, most likely because he speaks on his own authority without mentioning other teachers or even biblical proof texts. His teaching is interrupted by the appearance of a demon-possessed man. The unclean spirit knows who Jesus is ("the Holy One of God") and why he has come (to break the power of evil). When Jesus succeeds in expelling the demon, the onlookers are amazed by both his authoritative teaching and his powerful deeds. Thus his fame spreads throughout Galilee.

1:29–31. The second episode in Jesus' typical day occurs at the house of Simon (Peter) and Andrew. It involves Peter's mother-in-law, who is suffering from a fever. When informed of her condition, Jesus takes her by the hand and lifts her up. His touch is effective immediately and completely, so much so, that she gets up and serves her guests.

1:32–34. The third episode takes place in the evening, when "many" who are possessed by demons and suffering physical maladies are healed. As in 1:23–26, the demons know who Jesus is, and so Jesus prevents them from speaking. The reason for these commands to silence seems to be Mark's conviction that Jesus' true identity as the Messiah of Israel and the Son of God will be fully revealed only in the mystery of his cross and resurrection.

1:35–39. On the next day Jesus rises very early, goes out to a deserted place, and prays. The fact that Simon Peter and others pursue him—indicated by the verb "hunted, tracked down"—suggests that Jesus' followers misunderstand him. Apparently they want Jesus to exploit his growing popularity. Jesus, however, agrees to resume his ministry of teaching and healing on the grounds that "that is what I came out [from the Father] to do." His ministry moves quickly from Capernaum to the neighboring towns and throughout Galilee. In the early phases of his ministry Jesus teaches frequently in "their synagogues." After his rejection in the synagogue at Nazareth in 6:1–6, however, Jesus will teach elsewhere.

1:40–45. Jesus heals a leper. The way in which the leper approaches Jesus (begging, kneeling, and praying) suggests that he recognizes Jesus' divinity, while Jesus' own reactions (moved with pity, touching, and sternly warning) indicate Jesus' humanity. The biblical laws concerning leprosy (skin diseases thought to be communicable) are described in detail in Leviticus 13—14. Once more the healing is immediate and complete. As an observant Jew, Jesus sends the healed man to a priest in order to obtain an official declaration of his healing, and thus make possible his return to family and society. Despite Jesus' command to be silent, it appears that the healed man cannot resist spreading the word about Jesus, which makes it impossible for Jesus to travel in the towns of Galilee.

Controversy Stories

Mark 2:1—3:6 is a collection of controversy stories in which Jesus frustrates the opposition and wins the debates. Nevertheless, the opposition to him grows ever more intense. Various groups—scribes, Pharisees, and Herodians—try to trap Jesus, but through his cleverness and personal authority he eludes their plots. At the end, the Pharisees and Herodians join forces in order to destroy him.

2:1–12. The first controversy illustrates Jesus' authority both in word and in deed. It combines a healing account and a debate or controversy about forgiveness of sins. The story takes place in a house at Capernaum. People are so eager to see and hear Jesus that they crowd into the home. The only way the paralyzed man can reach Jesus for healing is for his four friends to take off the thatched roof and lower him down to Jesus inside the house. Jesus interprets their action as a testimony to their faith in his power to heal their paralyzed friend.

But when Jesus declares the man's sins to be forgiven, a controversy ensues among some scribes. They object that since only God can forgive sins, Jesus is usurping a divine privilege and so is committing blasphemy. By his question—"Which is easier, to say to the paralytic, 'Your sins are forgiven,' or to say, 'Stand up and take your mat and walk'?"—Jesus suggests that while it may be easier to say that someone's sins are forgiven (since there is no empirical proof either way), it is surely more difficult to empower a paralyzed man to walk (since there is empirical proof). In 2:10 Jesus identifies himself for the first time as "the Son of Man." To demonstrate his authority on both the physical and the spiritual levels, Jesus heals the man by his word alone: "I say to you, stand up, take your mat and go to your home." The healing is immediate and complete. The implication seems to be that if Jesus can heal merely by his word, he can also forgive sins by his word alone. The response of the crowd is wonder and admiration at what God is doing through Jesus.

2:13–17. The second controversy combines a "call" story and a debate with the scribes of the Pharisees. The call takes place by the seashore at Capernaum and involves a tax collector named Levi (who is called "Matthew" in Matthew 9:9). As a tax, or toll, collector, Levi is suspected of dishonesty and lack of patriotism because he is in the employ of Herod Antipas, and ultimately the Romans. Nevertheless, when Jesus says, "Follow me," Levi obeys immediately, just as the four fishermen did in 1:16–20.

By his occupation and perhaps by his conduct, Levi is regarded as a "sinner" by the scribes and Pharisees. In sharing a meal with tax collectors and sinners at Levi's house, Jesus disturbs the "scribes of the Pharisees." The scribes are experts in legal documents and in the interpretation and application of the Jewish Law, or Torah. The Pharisees comprise a religious movement within Judaism and are known for their knowledge and observance of the Torah. These scribes (who also happen to be Pharisees) are puzzled that a Jewish teacher like Jesus is spending so much time and effort with disreputable persons such as Levi.

Jesus responds that his mission from his Father is to work with those who need it most (sinners) rather than with the righteous—those who, at least in their own minds, are already in right relationship with God.

2:18–22. At the center of this collection of controversies is the one about fasting, along with two puzzling sayings about the old and the new. The controversy concerns devotional fasts practiced by John's disciples and the Pharisees, and the conspicuous absence of fasting among Jesus' disciples. Jesus' initial response in 2:19 consists of a question, and a restatement of it to the effect that no one fasts during a wedding celebration. Here Jesus assigns to himself a role assigned to God (the bridegroom) in the Old Testament as the spouse of Israel (see Isaiah 54:4–8; Hosea 2:16–20; etc.). The qualification in 2:20 that Jesus' followers will fast when he is "taken away" serves as a foreshadowing of Jesus' passion and death, as well as the basis for fasting among Jesus' later followers (see *Didache* 8:1). The sayings about old (garment, wineskins) and new (patch, wine) are linked loosely to the wedding imagery in 2:19–20 by their topics of clothing and wine. They highlight the new thing that is happening in and through Jesus, and its radical difference from the old.

Sabbath Observance

The two controversies in 2:23–28 and 3:1–6 concern Sabbath observance and, in particular, what constitutes work on the Sabbath. Refraining from manual labor on the Sabbath (our Saturday) was a distinctive feature (along with circumcision and ritual purity) among Jews in Jesus' time. According to Scripture, the Sabbath was a memorial of creation (Genesis 2:2) and of liberation from slavery in Egypt (Deuteronomy 5:14–15), and had a humanitarian dimension as well—a day of rest for all (Exodus 20:8–11).

2:23–28. The first Sabbath controversy has Jesus' disciples plucking heads of grain. While their action conforms to Deuteronomy 23:25, the Pharisees object that on the Sabbath this action is work and therefore forbidden. Jesus responds by appealing to David's example in 1 Samuel 21:1–6 in obtaining the "bread of the Presence" consecrated to God (see Leviticus 24:5–8) from the priest Ahimelech (not "Abiathar," as Mark has it). The point of the example seems to be that things consecrated to God, such as the loaves and the Sabbath, are not absolutes but exist for the good of humankind. This point is made explicit in Jesus' declaration, "The sabbath was made for humankind, and not humankind for the sabbath." There is some debate about whether Jesus' explanation, "so the Son of Man is lord even of the sabbath," refers only to Jesus or to humanity in general. More likely it refers to both, because Jesus as the Son of Man represents all of humanity.

3:1–6. The second Sabbath controversy combines a healing story and a controversy (as in 2:1–12). It takes place in the synagogue at Capernaum. The person who needs healing is a man with a withered hand, which is presumably a longtime condition and not life-threatening. The issue is whether Jesus' healing him on the Sabbath constitutes work. The opponents seem to be Pharisees who are trying to find reasons to bring legal charges against Jesus. The logic of Jesus' defense in 3:4 seems to be that if it is lawful to save a life on the Sabbath, so it must also be lawful to do good on the Sabbath, and that healing the man's withered hand would surely be doing good. Jesus' reaction to the opponents is highly emotional: "He looked around at them with anger; he was grieved at their hardness of heart." Again the healing is immediate and complete, the result of the man merely stretching out his hand in response to Jesus' command. However, in contrast to the amazement displayed by the onlookers in 2:12, the response of the Pharisees here in 3:6 is to enter a plot with the Herodians (supporters of the Herod dynasty) to destroy Jesus (see 12:13). So from the start Jesus' wise teachings and powerful healings meet resistance and hostility among his own people.

For Reflection and Discussion

What are the most important things you have learned from the prologue (Mark 1:1–13), and how will it influence your approach to the whole Gospel?

Imagine yourself as a resident of Capernaum during Jesus' "typical day." What do you see? What do you hear? How do you respond?

What elements of misunderstanding and hostility toward Jesus do you detect in this first part of Mark's Gospel?

3

Jesus' Authority Is Challenged in Galilee

Mark 3:7—6:6

The summary passage in Mark 3:7–12 is the transition, or bridge, between the first two major sections of Mark's Gospel (1:1—3:6 and 3:13—6:6). In both sections the two great themes are the manifestation of Jesus' authority and the growing opposition to him. Whereas in the former section the first theme dominated, in the second section there is more emphasis on the hostility that Jesus attracts.

3:7–12. Jesus withdraws from the synagogue to the seashore, presumably in order to avoid the plot by the Pharisees and Herodians in 3:6. Nevertheless, Jesus begins to gain even greater attention all over the Holy Land and beyond. Instead of his going out from Capernaum, now the crowds come to him. The popular interest in Jesus seems to revolve around his ability as a healer and exorcist. So great is the crush of the crowd that Jesus requests a boat from which he can teach while escaping the mob on the shore (see 4:1–2). As in 1:24 and 1:34, the demons recognize and confess that Jesus is the Son of God. Jesus orders

He left that place and came to his hometown, and his disciples followed him. On the Sabbath he began to teach in the synagogue, and many who heard him were astounded. They said, "Where did this man get all this? What is this wisdom that has been given to him? What deeds of power are being done by his hands! Is not this the carpenter, the son of Mary and brother of James and Joses and Judas and Simon, and are not his sisters here with us?" And they took offense at him. Then Jesus said to them, "Prophets are not without honor, except in their hometown, and among their own kin, and in their own house." And he could do no deed of power there, except that he laid his hands on a few sick people and cured them. And he was amazed at their unbelief.

—Mark 6:1–6

them to be silent because this is not yet the time for his true identity to be made public. That will come during the passion narrative, as the mystery of the cross unfolds.

3:13–19. Jesus' choosing of the twelve apostles takes place on a mountain, which in the Bible is often the site of divine revelations and encounters with God. Now away from the crowds, Jesus summons seven more disciples, bringing the number to twelve. The number twelve, of course, evokes the tradition of the twelve tribes of Israel and fits with Jesus' program for a renewed people of God. The twelve apostles are called to be with Jesus and to share in his mission of proclaiming God's kingdom and healing those possessed by demons. In other words, they are to do what Jesus himself has been doing throughout the first section of the Gospel.

The first three apostles listed—Simon (Peter), James, and John—were among the first disciples Jesus called and will form the inner circle at certain points as the Gospel proceeds (5:35–43; 9:2; 13:3; and 14:33). While the nickname "Peter" applied to Simon is clear enough ("the rock"), the epithet applied to James and John ("the sons of thunder") remains a mystery. From Mark's Gospel alone little is known about the other members of the Twelve, though the other canonical Gospels and the apocryphal Gospels supply further information.

Serious Accusations

3:20–35. Mark combines, in his typical "sandwich" technique, stories of Jesus' family's suspicions about his mental state and the scribes' charge that Jesus is possessed and

works through Satan's power. When Jesus returns "home" to Capernaum, again he draws a large crowd. His relatives decide to come from Nazareth to restrain him because they have heard rumors that he has gone crazy. (For more on the family of Jesus at Nazareth, see 6:1–6.)

Meanwhile, some scribes from Jerusalem charge that Jesus is possessed by a demon, and that he performs his exorcisms and healings out of demonic power. The opponents acknowledge that Jesus does perform exorcisms and healings. Their problem concerns the source or origin of Jesus' power to do so. In responding to their charges and exposing the illogical nature of their position, Jesus uses "parables," that is, analogies taken from everyday life (see 4:1–34). If Jesus were an instrument of Satan, then Satan's house and Satan's kingdom would be divided and so could not stand for long. Also, by exorcising demons, Jesus is effectively overpowering Satan ("the strong man") and showing himself to be "the stronger one." Finally, in 3:28–30 Jesus defines the unforgivable sin as the failure to discern that the Holy Spirit is at work in his ministry of exorcism and healing.

Then members of Jesus' family arrive at Capernaum and ask to see him. Instead of acceding to their request, Jesus redefines his family as those who dedicate themselves to doing the will of God. Such persons are Jesus' true brothers and sisters.

A Lengthy Speech

In Mark's Gospel Jesus gives two substantial speeches: the parables about God's kingdom (4:1–34), and the eschatological discourse—or, discussion of end times (13:1–37). With 4:1–2 Mark sets the scene by the Sea of Galilee, with a large crowd on the shore and Jesus sitting in a boat a little off shore (see 3:9).

4:3–9. The first parable is known generally as the parable of the sower. This parable is bracketed by a call to listen carefully. The real focus of this parable is not so much the one who sows but the four kinds of soil and the four sowings. The first sowing takes place on the road, and the seeds get eaten immediately by birds. The second sowing on rocky ground allows some growth but fails quickly due to the soil's lack of depth. The seeds sown among thorns start well enough but quickly get choked off. While in all three sowings so far there is a gradual increase in growth, they all end in failure. However, the fourth and final sowing in good soil produces spectacular results and a superabundant harvest. This is emphasized not only by the huge numbers but also by the verbs "growing up and increasing and yielding." The parable promises that even though Jesus' preaching of God's kingdom will meet some opposition and failure, in the end the final result—the fullness of God's kingdom—will be overwhelmingly successful.

4:10–12. Jesus explains that he teaches in parables. In his private instruction to the Twelve and others, Jesus states that while to them God has revealed through him the "secret" of God's kingdom (that is, the unfolding of the divine plan leading up to the kingdom's fullness), to outsiders that mystery is cast in figurative speech, or parables. The word *parable* comes from the Greek word *paraballo*, meaning "place beside." It is a kind of analogy that compares something well known to something less known but more important. Taking his biblical rationale from Isaiah 6:9–10 about the hardening of people's hearts,

Jesus foresees that as the prophet of God's kingdom he, too, will meet misunderstanding and failure.

4:13–20. The sower parable is interpreted. Jesus explains that in this parable, he is the sower and the seeds are his preaching about God's kingdom. The soils are the different kinds of persons who are exposed to Jesus' preaching. The seed sown on the roadway gets snatched away by Satan. The seed sown on rocky ground falls away when trouble or persecution comes along. The seed sown among the thorns gets choked by "the cares of the world, and the lure of wealth, and the desire for other things." By contrast the seed sown in good soil yields a spectacular harvest. The ideal recipients of Jesus' message "hear the word and accept it and bear fruit." The vocabulary and the situations sketched in this interpretation seem to reflect the experience of the early church, and may not have come directly from Jesus but developed in the faith community and became part of the tradition recorded by Mark. Nevertheless, the interpretation is an accurate reading of Jesus' parable and an appropriate application of it to real experience. In its present position, this explanation occupies a central place in Jesus' discourse about God's kingdom.

4:21–25. Jesus promises that the mystery of God's kingdom will eventually be revealed, and that those who receive it positively will be greatly rewarded. His sayings here match those in 4:10–12 in the structure of the parables discourse. The parable in 4:21 suggests that a lamp fulfills its purpose only when it is placed on a lampstand and is used to illuminate a room. Likewise, the purpose of Jesus' preaching about God's kingdom is to disclose the divine mystery that will surely come to light

(4:22). The proverbs in 4:24–25 are variations on the theme that the rich get richer and the poor get poorer. This harsh reality applies not only in the sphere of economics but also in the intellectual and spiritual life. That piece of wisdom was already indicated in the parable of the sower (4:3–9, 13–20).

4:26–29 and 4:30–32. These two seed parables complement the earlier seed parable in 4:3–9. In fact, all three seed parables may have circulated as a unit in the early Jesus tradition and fit well, in their form and content, with what we know about Jesus' own teaching. By their introductory formulas it is clear that both concern the kingdom of God. The parable of the seed growing by itself contrasts the small beginnings of God's kingdom in Jesus' preaching and the gigantic harvest that it will eventually produce. In the meantime there is steady growth—an impression encouraged by the measured way in which the story is told. However, the cause of the growth remains mysterious, at least to the farmer. The message is that God will bring about the fullness of his kingdom in God's own time and way. Once more, the parable provides encouragement and hope in the face of misunderstanding and hostility. The parable of the mustard seed makes similar points about God's kingdom. This tiny seed grows mysteriously into a large bush (perhaps six feet tall). Likewise the tiny seeds of God's kingdom being sown by Jesus in his preaching and healing ministry will issue in the fullness of God's kingdom. God will bring about the kingdom in God's own time and way. Meanwhile, we can be sure that it is now growing among us and will eventually come into its fullness.

4:33–34. Mark's conclusion of this section matches the introduction in 4:1–2. It explains that Jesus used analogies (parables) from everyday experience to teach the crowds about God's kingdom (the fullness of which is future and transcendent). Mark also notes that Jesus gave fuller explanations to his disciples in private (as in 4:10–12; 7:17–23; 10:10–12; and 10:23–30).

Miracle Stories

The miracle stories in 4:35—5:43 (the stilling of the storm, the exorcism of the possessed man, the healing of the woman with the flow of blood, and the restoration of Jairus's daughter to life) illustrate Jesus' power over nature, demons, disease, and death.

4:35–41. In stilling the storm at sea, Jesus does what in the Old Testament only God can do (Psalm 89:9; 106:9; Isaiah 51:9–10). The day of parables ends, and Jesus and his disciples move by boat from the western (Jewish) shore to the eastern (Gentile) shore of the Sea of Galilee. The boat had served as the stage for Jesus' discourse on God's kingdom (4:1–2). During the voyage a great storm comes up, and the disciples are in danger of drowning. Jesus, however, manages to sleep through the storm. In waking him, the disciples address him as "Teacher" and express some impatience at his apparent lack of concern. When Jesus springs into action, he rebukes the wind and commands the sea to be quiet, as if he were expelling a demon (see 1:25). The return to calm is immediate and complete, just as in most of Jesus' exorcisms and healings. In the aftermath Jesus criticizes his disciples for their fear (in the negative sense of cowardice), and questions their trust in God and in him, "Have you still no faith?" From this point in Mark's overall narrative, the disciples will frequently prove to be negative examples of "no faith." Against their bad example, the positive and heroic conduct of Jesus as the faithful Son of God will shine brightly. In response to what they have just witnessed, the disciples in 4:41 exhibit another (more positive) form of fear ("awe") and raise the kind of question that runs throughout Mark's Gospel: "Who then is this, that even the wind and sea obey him?" The stilling of the storm suggests that since Jesus does what only God can do, he is in some sense divine.

5:1–20. Jesus' healing of the possessed man in Gerasa demonstrates his power over demons. The narrative is long and vivid, and sometimes confusing. Having arrived safely on the eastern (Gentile) shore, Jesus and his disciples land in Gerasa. (The problem is that Gerasa is more than thirty-five miles from the sea.) Jesus meets a man possessed by demons, who is acting in bizarre ways, shows extraordinary strength, and lives in the burial caves. Then Jesus encounters the demons. As in 1:24 and 1:34, they know that Jesus is the "Son of the Most High God." By learning that the demon's name is "Legion," Jesus gains power over him and is able to expel him. (In the Roman army a legion had six thousand men. Some interpreters see this as an anti-Roman reference.) In accord with the demons' request, Jesus sends them into a herd of pigs that rushes to a cliff, falls into the water, and drowns. (For Jews pigs were unclean animals, and they would have found the pigs' demise a great joke.) Then the local residents are amazed to find the man properly dressed and in his right mind. Nevertheless, they beg Jesus to leave their territory. It's not clear whether they are afraid of losing more pigs or just overwhelmed by Jesus' display of power.

When the healed man asks to become a disciple (to "be with him"), Jesus advises him to return home and tell his friends how the Lord has shown mercy to him. This is a departure from Jesus' practice of demanding silence from those he heals. The result is that Jesus' fame as a healer spreads throughout the ten cities (the Decapolis) in the largely Gentile region on the eastern side of the Sea of Galilee.

5:21–43. Even longer and almost as vivid is the account of Jesus' healing of the woman with the flow of blood and his resuscitation of Jairus's daughter. Taken together in Mark's characteristic sandwich technique, they demonstrate Jesus' sovereignty over disease and death. When Jesus and his disciples return to the western (Jewish) side of the Sea of Galilee, he is approached by a Jewish leader named Jairus, who begs him to heal his daughter, who is near death. He wants Jesus to lay his hands on her, thus transferring God's blessing and his healing power to her.

On his way to Jairus's house, Jesus encounters a woman who has suffered with a flow of blood for twelve years. Her chronic condition has left her physically ill, ritually impure, and financially impoverished. Her only hope is to touch Jesus' garment in the hope that his healing power might be transferred to her. When she does so, her healing is immediate and complete. When Jesus discovers what has happened and who touched his garment, he attributes the woman's healing to her faith: "Your faith has made you well."

When Jesus learns that Jairus's daughter has died, he refuses to turn back and reassures Jairus by saying, "Do not fear, only believe." When he and three disciples who make up the inner circle (Peter, James, and John) arrive at the house, they find great commotion, which is heightened by the laments and other rituals of mourning. When Jesus suggests that "the child is not dead but sleeping," he is greeted with laughter and ridicule. But Jesus persists, and brings the girl's parents and the three disciples into the room where her corpse is laid out. There Jesus takes her hand, commands her to get up, and restores her to life. Again the healing is immediate and complete, and the girl begins to walk around and eventually eats a meal. The result is amazement on the part of the bystanders, and once more Jesus issues a command to be silent about what they have seen. Jesus' restoration of Jairus's daughter to life is a preview of his own resurrection (and ours).

6:1–6. Having shown his power over storms, demons, disease, and death, Jesus is nevertheless rejected by the people of his hometown in Nazareth. His authoritative teaching in the local synagogue at first impresses and even astounds the town's people. However, their enthusiasm cools as they begin to ask critical questions about the source of Jesus' wisdom and healing powers. And because they have known Jesus and his family for many years, they cannot believe that Jesus is now so special. (Their reference to him as the "son of Mary" may mean that Joseph was dead. Whether the brothers and sisters referred to here were cousins, half-siblings through Joseph, or full siblings, has been debated for many centuries.) Jesus comments on the negative reception he received by quoting what sounds like a proverb about prophets not being accepted in their own home area. Mark comments that Jesus "could do no deed of power there" due to the people's lack of faith in him. Just as the first major section in Mark's Gospel ended with the plot of the Herodians and the

Pharisees against Jesus, so the second section concludes with a comment about the unbelief of his former friends and neighbors, who thought they knew all there was to know about him.

For Reflection and Discussion

Trace the various indications of hostility toward Jesus in Mark 3:7—6:6. Who shows hostility, and why?

From Jesus' parables in 4:1–34, what do you learn about the kingdom of God?

What do the various miracle stories in 4:35—5:43 suggest about the identity of Jesus?

4

Jesus Is Misunderstood in Galilee and Beyond

Mark 6:6—8:21

Whereas early in the second major section of Mark's Gospel Jesus called the twelve apostles to be with him, here at the beginning of the third major section, he sends them out as extensions of his own mission. They are to do what he did and are to subordinate all their material concerns to the mission. Later they will return and report to Jesus what they have done. In between, Mark tells by way of flashback the story of John the Baptist's death (see 1:14). The "sandwich" structure is a reminder of the suffering that may be involved in carrying out the mission of proclaiming God's kingdom in word and deed.

Apostles Sent Out

6:6b–13. Jesus invites and empowers the twelve to do the kinds of things that he has done thus far in Mark's narrative: to proclaim repentance in the face of God's coming kingdom

51

The Pharisees came and began to argue with him, asking him for a sign from heaven, to test him. And he sighed deeply in his spirit and said, "Why does this generation ask for a sign? Truly I tell you, no sign will be given to this generation." And he left them, and getting into the boat again, he went across to the other side.

—Mark 8:11–13

(1:15), to cast out demons, and to heal the sick. In the Holy Land and in the whole Greco-Roman world, religions and philosophies were spread by traveling missionaries. Jesus insists that his missionaries take along only the bare necessities by way of baggage and clothing, lest they be mistaken for the charlatans who were common in the ancient world. Moreover, they are not to spend time and energy seeking to improve their lodgings. Rather, they must accept the hospitality initially offered to them, and also accept rejection in a nonviolent way.

6:14–29. Mark depicts King Herod as fascinated by Jesus and convinced that he is John the Baptist brought back to life. This Herod is Herod Antipas, a son of Herod the Great, and the ruler in Galilee. The various theories about Jesus' identity—John, Elijah, or a prophet—recur in 8:27–30. It is Herod who executed John the Baptist. According to Mark, Herod Antipas had married Herodias, the wife of his brother Philip, and in doing so he had transgressed the biblical prohibition against such a marriage (see Leviticus 18:16; 20:21). (The details of the marriage were even more complicated than Mark indicates.) As a prophet John protested this illegal and immoral union. John's protest seems to have affected Herodias more than Herod Antipas, who appears to have been fascinated by John.

John's death is described in gruesome detail. At Herod's birthday banquet, with the elite of Galilee in attendance, the daughter of Herodias performed a dance that greatly pleased Herod. (The girl may have been quite young, and the dance need not have been erotic in any way.) So pleased was Herod that he foolishly promised to give the girl anything she wanted, up to half his kingdom—which was not even his to give away. At her mother's urging, the girl asked for the head of John the Baptist. Having made this promise in front of all his guests, Herod could not go back on his word without incurring public shame. Despite his great interest in John, Herod ordered him to be beheaded and to have his head brought on a serving dish to Herodias and her daughter. The care that John's disciples displayed for his corpse in 6:29 anticipates what will happen with Jesus' body in 15:45–46.

6:30–32. The apostles return from their mission and report to Jesus about their activities of exorcism and healing. Thus they fulfill Mark's ideal of discipleship as being with Jesus and sharing in his mission. Jesus suggests that they all go to a "deserted place" for rest and relaxation. However, their vacation plans get interrupted by a large crowd that will need to be fed.

Famous Miracles

6:33–44. Jesus' feeding of the five thousand contrasts sharply with the dissolute and gruesome banquet presided over by Herod Antipas. Despite his plans for rest in a "deserted place," the crowd learns of his movements and arrives at the deserted place before Jesus does. Out of compassion for them, Jesus teaches them "because they were like sheep without a shepherd," a rich biblical image expressing God's care for his people (see Psalm 23). The late hour and the largeness of the crowd set the stage for Jesus' miraculous feeding. When the disciples suggest that Jesus dismiss the crowd so that they might get food on their own, Jesus proposes that they feed the crowd. This seems impossible; feeding such a crowd would be very expensive (two hundred days' wages), and the only food at their disposal is five loaves of bread and two fish. Jesus takes the initiative and has the crowd sit on the grass in ordered groups. Then he takes the bread, says the traditional blessing, and has the disciples distribute bread and fish to the entire crowd. The miracle is that all eat and have their fill, while there is still a large amount of leftovers. The twelve baskets of leftovers suggest a connection with the twelve tribes of Israel. Only at the end do we learn that the crowd numbered five thousand men. The second multiplication of food for four thousand persons in 8:1–10 probably envisions a Gentile audience. Also, the way in which Jesus' actions are described points toward Jesus' Last Supper with his disciples in 14:22–25.

6:45–52. The miraculous feeding is followed by a rescue at sea, during which Jesus' divine character is once more revealed (see 4:35–41; 9:2–8). After dismissing the crowd and directing his disciples to go toward Bethsaida, Jesus goes to a mountain to pray (see 1:35). In the meantime, early in the morning (3:00 to 6:00 A.M.), heavy winds come up on the lake, and the disciples find themselves in trouble. They see Jesus coming toward them walking on the sea. In the Old Testament the image of God walking on the sea (Job 9:8; Psalm 77:19) symbolizes God's sovereignty over the powers of chaos threatening the created order. In identifying himself as "it is I," Jesus uses a familiar biblical formula used by God (especially in Isaiah 40—55). When the storm subsides (as in 4:35–41), the disciples are astounded at what they have witnessed. Nevertheless, they still do not fully comprehend who Jesus is.

6:53–56. The description of Jesus' many healings recalls similar healings earlier in the story through the use of now-familiar words and phrases, such as "mats" (2:1–12), "begged" (1:40–45), and "touch even the fringe of his garment" (5:24b–34). These healings take place on the western shore, at Gennesaret—the territory between Capernaum and Tiberias. Jesus goes to where the people are, in villages, cities, and farms; and he meets them in marketplaces. The enthusiasm of the crowd is at a high level; there is firm belief in Jesus' power to heal; and those who touch even his garments find healing.

Disputes about Legal Matters

The disputes about various legal matters concern the tradition of the elders, the specific practice of "Corban," and ritual and moral purity. The audience for the first two segments consists of Pharisees and scribes, while the audience for the third part is first the crowd and then the disciples.

7:1–8. The Pharisees and scribes are disturbed on noticing that some of Jesus' disciples fail to observe their custom of washing hands before eating. The issue here is more ritual purity than hygiene. Mark provides an explanation for non-Jews about some of the Jewish customs pertaining to ritual purity. The Pharisees in particular sought to extend some of the rules pertaining to priests in the temple to all Israelites. The target of Jesus' critique here is "the tradition of the elders"—that is, the customs and regulations the Pharisees and scribes were devising to more specifically interpret and apply the Law of Moses. Using the biblical text from Isaiah 29:13, Jesus accuses them of "teaching human precepts as doctrines," and of putting their traditions above the Law itself.

7:9–13. Jesus gives an example of their abandoning a commandment of God in order to observe one of their traditions. According to the Law of Moses, one must honor one's parents (Exodus 20:12) and never speak evil of them (Exodus 21:17). The word *Corban* means "gift" or "offering." The case described in 7:11 involves designating a large sum of money or a piece of property to be dedicated to the upkeep of the temple. Such an apparently pious action might have the effect of depriving one's parents of their right to be supported by their son's money or property. Jesus interprets this custom—not found in the Hebrew Bible but presumably allowed or encouraged by the scribes and Pharisees—as an example of letting a human tradition override a biblical commandment.

7:14–23. Jesus returns to the topic of ritual purity. He declares to the crowd that what defiles a person is not what goes into the mouth (food) but what comes out (words and actions). Thus he places moral purity ahead of ritual purity. Then he provides private instructions for the disciples (see 4:10–12, 34; 10:10–12; 10:23–31). Jesus' annoyance at his disciples' failure to understand in 7:18 prepares for his even more extreme exasperation in 8:17–21. Then Jesus repeats his statement and expands upon it. It is not so much what goes into a person that defiles, as it is what comes out of the heart (understood as both intellect and emotion). Mark's parenthetical comment ("Thus he declared all foods clean") probably goes further than Jesus went on the matter. Otherwise it would not have been such a point of contention in early Christian circles (see Acts 15 and Galatians 2:11–14). As examples of moral defilement Jesus offers a list of twelve vices in 7:21–22: fornication, theft, murder, and so on. For similar lists, see Galatians 5:19–21; Romans 1:29–31; 1 Corinthians 6:9–10; 1 Timothy 1:9–10; and 2 Timothy 3:2–4. For a list of Christian virtues (the "fruit of the Spirit"), see Galatians 5:22–23: love, joy, peace, and so on.

Three Episodes among the Gentiles

7:24–30. Jesus' healing of the Syrophoenician woman's daughter takes place in the vicinity of Tyre, a Gentile city on the Mediterranean coast (in present-day Lebanon) and an enemy of ancient Israel. Once more his plans for solitude are changed when a woman whose daughter is possessed by a demon ("an unclean spirit") approaches him in the hope of obtaining healing for her. She is identified as a non-Jew ("a Gentile [literally, a Greek] of Syrophoenician origin"). In response to her plea, Jesus answers her in an uncharacteristically harsh way: "Let the children be fed first, for it is not fair to take the children's food and throw it to dogs." The "children" here are Jews, and the "dogs" are Gentiles. Thus Jesus not only asserts that his mission is primarily for his fellow Jews, but also insults the woman and all Gentiles, especially since in the ancient world dogs were not so much pets as they were scavengers. Rather than being discouraged by the insult, the women responds by addressing Jesus with a respectful "Sir" and observes that even dogs are allowed to eat scraps from the table.

In this verbal duel the Gentile woman gets the better of Jesus, appears to change his mind, and makes him relent. It is possible to read this interchange as Jesus' attempt to test the woman's faith. But it is even more likely that the woman's display of faith broadened Jesus' outlook and the scope of his ministry. On the strength of the woman's persistent display of faith in Jesus' power to heal, Jesus dismisses her with the assurance that her daughter is already healed. On returning home she finds it just as Jesus had promised.

7:31–37. Jesus' healing of a deaf and mute man also takes place in Gentile territory, in the Decapolis—the constellation of largely Gentile cities east of the Sea of Galilee. The people there present as a candidate for healing a deaf man who speaks with difficulty. Whereas in most healing stories Jesus cures immediately by word alone, here he engages in a complex ritual that borders on magic. Jesus first places his fingers in the man's ears. Next he spits and touches his tongue. (In some circles saliva was thought to have healing power.) Then he utters the Aramaic word *Ephphatha*, which means "Be opened." The result is that the man hears and even speaks plainly. When Jesus orders the witnesses to be silent about the miracle, it has the opposite effect (as in 1:44–45). The reason for the command to silence seems to be that only with Jesus' death and resurrection does his true identity become clear. The crowd's cry of joy ("he even makes the deaf to hear and the mute to speak") evokes the hopes of Jews returning from exile in Babylon in the sixth century B.C. (Isaiah 35:5–6).

8:1–10. Also in Gentile territory is the feeding of the four thousand. It is quite similar to the feeding of the five thousand in

6:33–44, which clearly took place in Jewish territory. Here Jesus himself recognizes the problem of feeding such a large crowd and shows compassion for their hunger (rather than judgment for their lack of sound leadership). When the disciples inform Jesus about seven loaves and a few small fish, he gives thanks to God and has the disciples distribute the food. The result is that all are fed and filled, and there are even seven baskets of leftovers. Again, the miracle of the feeding points forward to the Last Supper (14:22–25). The exact location of Dalmanutha in 8:10 remains a puzzle, though the presence of Pharisees in 8:11–13 indicates that it was on the western (Jewish) side of the Sea of Galilee.

8:11–13. Despite the mighty works Jesus has done, the Pharisees demand a further authenticating sign from God that Jesus really is the prophet and Messiah sent from God. We can assume that the Pharisees wanted a more direct and dramatic manifestation of God than they already had witnessed in Jesus' healings, exorcisms, and other miracles. Out of exasperation, Jesus declares that "no sign will be given [by God] to this generation." The conversation is over, and Jesus rejoins his disciples in the boat.

8:14–21. The disciples' misunderstanding about the bread arises from bringing only one loaf in the boat. Jesus takes the occasion to warn them against the "yeast of the Pharisees" and the "yeast of Herod." Beside its positive effect in flour (see Matthew 13:33), yeast or leaven can have a corruptive effect in making bread stale or moldy. The "yeast of the Pharisees" may refer specifically to their demand for an authenticating sign or to their general opposition to Jesus throughout the Gospel. The "yeast of

Herod" may refer to the Herodians' part in the plot against Jesus and/or Herod Antipas's role in having John executed (6:14–29).

The disciples, however, fail to make the connections. In response to their misunderstanding, Jesus berates the disciples for their obtuseness regarding the two multiplications of the loaves. With a series of pointed questions Jesus exposes their failure to understand him. The first major section of Mark's Gospel ended with a plot against Jesus by the Pharisees and Herodians (3:6). The second section concluded with the rejection of Jesus by the people of his hometown (6:1–6). The third section climaxes with Jesus' own disciples misunderstanding him (8:14–21). To understand Jesus properly, they (and we) need to make the journey with Jesus up to Jerusalem, and to confront the mystery of his death and resurrection.

For Reflection and Discussion

Imagine that you are one of the disciples who witness the feeding of the five thousand and then see Jesus' power over the sea. You have already seen him heal the sick. How do these larger events begin to change your perception of him?

Why do you think Jesus taught in parables and explained their meaning only to the disciples? Can you see any strategy there?

Jesus points out how the Pharisees' legalism gets in the way of truly fulfilling God's law. What examples of legalism do you find today among Christians?

How were the miraculous feedings similar to what we experience in the Eucharist?

They went on from there and passed through Galilee. He did not want anyone to know it; for he was teaching his disciples, saying to them, "The Son of Man is to be betrayed into human hands, and they will kill him, and three days after being killed, he will rise again." But they did not understand what he was saying and were afraid to ask him.

—Mark 9:30–32

5

Jesus' Instructions on the Way to Jerusalem

Mark 8:22—10:52

At the center of Mark's Gospel is the journey of Jesus and his disciples from northern Galilee to Jerusalem. This section is introduced and concluded by the healing of a blind man. Along the way there are three predictions of Jesus' death and resurrection. After each of the three predictions there is a misunderstanding on the disciples' part. This provides Jesus with the opportunity to correct the misunderstanding and offer more teachings about who he is (Christology) and what it means to follow him (discipleship). On this journey Jesus makes clear the challenge involved in following him, and the Transfiguration provides a preview of the glory that awaits him and his followers.

A Different Kind of Messiah

8:22–26. The initial healing of a blind man takes place at Bethsaida, on the northeast corner of the Sea of Galilee. By bringing the blind man to Jesus, the people there display faith in his power to heal. This healing occurs gradually, in two phases. Jesus engages in a healing ritual, something like that in 7:33. He brings the man outside the village, applies saliva to his eyes, and lays his hands on him. However, the result is only partially successful, and the man does not yet see clearly. Jesus again lays hands on him, and this time the healing is immediate and complete. In sending him home without returning to the village, Jesus renews the theme of the "messianic secret." Taken as a whole, this episode symbolizes the gradual process involved in coming to understand Jesus' teaching and healing in light of the mystery of the cross.

8:27–30. The journey from Galilee to Jerusalem begins with Peter's confession of Jesus as the Messiah. This takes place at Caesarea Philippi, in northern Israel, a site connected in some circles with divine revelations. When Jesus asks his disciples about how people perceive him, the three answers he gets are those already mentioned in 6:14–15: John the Baptist restored to life (Jesus was associated with John), Elijah (the prophet expected to return before the full coming of God's kingdom, see 9:9–13), or one of the prophets (perhaps even the prophet like Moses as in Deuteronomy 18:15–18). When Jesus asks his disciples directly, Peter speaks on behalf of the group (as in 8:32; 9:5; 10:28; 11:21) and identifies Jesus as the Messiah.

There were several different understandings of the Messiah among Jews in Jesus' time. One approach looked for a powerful descendant of David who would serve as warrior, political leader, and judge, and so restore Israel's fortunes among the nations (see

Psalms of Solomon 17). The disciples had to learn that Jesus was not that kind of Messiah. Of course, a warrior Messiah would be a threat to the Roman and the Jewish authorities. In this context, Jesus' command that people be silent about his work and identity made good sense.

8:31–38. Jesus' first prediction of the passion is followed by Peter's misunderstanding of—and Jesus' correction and instruction about—the cost of discipleship. What the disciples must come to accept is that Jesus is a suffering Messiah, something almost no one expects. Having accepted Peter's confession of him as the Messiah, Jesus explains what kind of Messiah he is. He identifies himself as the Son of Man and prophesies his rejection, death, and resurrection. Peter refuses to accept the idea of Jesus as a suffering Messiah, and Jesus in turn rebukes him for thinking only in human terms. Peter's failure to accept the mystery of the cross is corrected and balanced by sayings about following Jesus. These sayings concern the challenge to take up the cross, losing and gaining one's life/soul, the extraordinary value of one's life/soul, and the importance of not being ashamed of the Son of Man.

9:1–13. The transfiguration is a preview of the glory that Jesus will enjoy in his resurrected life and in the fullness of God's kingdom. It is preceded by a transitional saying (9:1) and followed by a conversation about the second coming of Elijah (9:9–13). In Mark's context, those who will not taste death are Peter, James, and John. The promise that they will see the kingdom of God come with power is fulfilled in part in the Transfiguration, and then even more dramatically in Jesus' resurrection and in the fullness of God's kingdom.

The Transfiguration takes place on a high mountain, known in ancient times as the place of divine encounters and revelations. It occurs in the presence of Jesus' inner circle, three of the first disciples he called. There on the mountain, Jesus undergoes a metamorphosis, and he shines in brilliance. Then he enters into conversation with Moses and Elijah, who represent the Law and the Prophets. In his usual role as spokesman, Peter suggests (somewhat awkwardly) constructing tents or booths for all three figures, perhaps as a way of prolonging the experience. The voice from the cloud (a symbol of divine presence) echoes the heavenly voice heard at Jesus' baptism and identifies Jesus as the beloved Son of God. Suddenly the whole experience is over.

While coming down from the mountain, Jesus orders his three disciples to be silent about what they have witnessed until the Son of Man (Jesus) has risen from the dead. What most likely puzzled the disciples was not the idea of resurrection (with which they would have been familiar) but rather the notion that one person might undergo resurrection before the full coming of God's kingdom. The topic shifts in 9:11–13 to the prophecy in Malachi 4:5–6 about Elijah returning before the full coming of God's kingdom. On the one hand, Jesus warns that the Son of Man must suffer before Elijah comes. On the other hand, he identifies John the Baptist with Elijah and so implies that Elijah has already come.

9:14–29. The account of the healing of the possessed boy is distinctive for its many details and its length. The major theme running through this story is faith. The first part introduces the many characters and focuses on the disciples' failure to exorcise the demon and heal the boy. (The detailed description of the boy's symptoms led Matthew in 17:15 to diagnose the condition as epilepsy, literally, being "moonstruck.") Jesus' judgment on the whole situation is that it was a sign of the "faithless generation" in which they all lived. In the second part, Jesus witnesses the boy's symptoms for himself and learns that he has been suffering with them since childhood. When the boy's father asks Jesus for help ("if you are able"), Jesus assures him that "all things can be done for the one who believes." In response the boy's father issues his memorable profession: "I believe; help my unbelief!" Then Jesus performs the exorcism successfully despite the demon's struggle, and in a sentence full of resurrection language he raises up the boy and makes him stand on his own. Finally, in another private conversation, Jesus explains to his disciples why they were not able to cast out the demon: "This kind can come out only through prayer."

Teachings for the Disciples

The rest of Jesus' teachings in Galilee are directed to his disciples. In 10:1 he will go to Judea and teach publicly again.

9:30–32. In the second passion prediction, Jesus refers to himself as the Son of Man. "Is to be betrayed" indicates that Jesus is predicting Judas's actions, though the phrase could also refer to the unfolding of the divine plan. This is the shortest of the three passion predictions. The comment that the disciples did not understand it is surprising in light of the previous passion prediction in 8:31. From now on, the disciples often serve as negative examples whose obtuseness contrasts with Jesus' foresight.

9:33–37. The depth of the disciples' misunderstanding is revealed by their dispute about greatness within their circle. This incident takes place in Capernaum, "in the house" (Peter's?). In a status-conscious and honor-shame society, the topic of greatness within a group or village was a major concern. By his saying in 9:35 and symbolic action in 9:36–37, Jesus subverts the assumptions on which such a society was built. In Jesus' movement, greatness consists in the service to others (see 10:43–45). By welcoming a child, Jesus elevates the status of someone who in a hierarchical-patriarchal society had little or no importance. Indeed, Jesus goes so far as to insert the child into the hierarchy that extends from God the Father through Jesus the Son to humankind.

9:38–41. The episode of the exorcist is linked to the preceding incident by its emphasis on the name of Jesus (see "in my name" in 9:37). It appears that someone was performing exorcisms while using the name of Jesus as a kind of magical instrument. Only here in Mark's Gospel does John serve as the spokesman for the disciples. Whereas the disciples tried to stop the strange exorcist, Jesus displays a remarkably tolerant attitude: "Whoever is not against us is for us" (compare Matthew 12:30 and Luke 11:23). While the saying in 9:41 refers to using the name of Jesus, it concerns a different topic: strangers who perform acts of kindness for disciples.

9:42–48. In Greek, a *skandalon* is an "obstacle" or "stumbling block" that trips up someone along the way. Here it serves as the keyword for the saying (9:42), which warns that it would be better for those who cause simple believers to stumble to be drowned at sea than to face punishment from God. The three sayings in 9:43–48 warn that it would be better for those who allow their hands, feet, or eyes, respectively, to cause themselves to stumble to cut off the offending member than to endure the eternal punishments they deserve.

9:49–50. These three sayings feature the word "salt." They allude to different properties or uses of salt: as a purifying agent, as a seasoning and a preservative, and as an element in making covenants and offering sacrifices.

10:1–12. Jesus and his disciples arrive in Judea (while avoiding Samaria), and he resumes teaching in public. He engages in a debate with some Pharisees over the legality of divorce. Mark describes this encounter as a test, since divorce was permitted in the Old Testament and since the Pharisees most likely knew about Jesus' radical teaching already. In their conversation Jesus elicits from the Pharisees the one text that allowed divorce (Deuteronomy 24:1–4) and interprets that text as a concession to the hardness of the human heart. Instead he points to two passages from Genesis 1—2 (before the Fall) as expressing God's original intention regarding marriage: God made them "male and female" (Genesis 1:27), and "they become one flesh" (Genesis 2:24). Thus Jesus appears to abrogate the husband's right to divorce his wife, and to hold up lifetime monogamy as the divinely inspired ideal. (For a slightly different presentation of this episode with an exception for "unchastity," see Matthew 19:1–9. See also the exceptions made in Matthew 5:32 and 1 Corinthians 7:12–16.) Then in a private instruction to his disciples, Jesus forbids divorce and remarriage for both husbands and wives (see also Luke 16:18).

10:13–16. While flowing naturally from the passage about marriage and divorce, Jesus' blessing of the little children is really concerned with the kinds of persons who can enter God's kingdom. When the children are brought to receive Jesus' blessing, the disciples try to prevent them. Their action in turn angers Jesus (see 3:5; 8:12; 8:17–21; 9:19), presumably because it betrays a misunderstanding of him and his teaching about God's kingdom. Whereas in 9:36–37 the child signified lack of social status, here the children represent powerlessness, dependence, and receptivity. Only those who receive God's kingdom as a gift may enter it. In this context Jesus embraces the children, lays hands on them, and blesses them.

Riches and the Kingdom

Mark 10:17–31 consists of three sections that deal with various aspects of riches and poverty.

10:17–22. The first section portrays riches as an obstacle to discipleship. A man approaches Jesus and asks what he needs to do to inherit eternal life. Jesus tells him to keep the biblical commandments. When the man claims to have kept them since his youth, Jesus' mood changes from a testy defensiveness ("Why do you call me good?") to genuine affection. And so he issues an invitation to the man to become his disciple. But this will involve selling his possessions and giving the money to the poor. Only at the end do we learn that the man is rich and so does not accept Jesus' call.

10:23–27. The second section alludes to the privileged spiritual position of the economically poor by reflecting on

how hard it is for the rich to enter God's kingdom. This teaching puzzles the disciples, since they most likely regarded wealth as a blessing from God. The "camel through the eye of the needle" analogy suggests that it is almost impossible for the rich to enter God's kingdom, though shortly afterward Jesus acknowledges that "for God all things are possible."

10:28–31. The third section promises great rewards to those who give up their families and possessions to follow Jesus. In response to Peter's question, Jesus assures those who give up these things "for the sake of the good news" will receive even larger families and possessions in this age and eternal life in the age to come. He does, however, inject a sobering note into the list by the inclusion of the phrase "with persecutions."

On the Road to Jerusalem

10:32–34. Jesus prophesies what will happen in Jerusalem. Nevertheless, he willingly accepts his fate and moves relentlessly toward it. This third passion prediction is much more detailed than the other two (8:31; 9:31). The words of this prophecy provide an apt summary of Mark's Gospel story. Indeed, so much of it is echoed later in Mark 14—15, that it appears to have been composed or at least filled out by the Evangelist. Note that this passage places ultimate responsibility for Jesus' death on the Romans: "then they will hand him over to the Gentiles."

10:35–40. The depth of the disciples' misunderstanding is manifested in James and John's request to have places of special prominence when Jesus comes into his glory. It's as if they have not been listening to the passion prediction and to Jesus' teaching throughout the journey. Instead of granting their request, Jesus challenges them to drink the cup he will drink and undergo the baptism he will undergo. Here Jesus evokes the biblical image of the "cup of suffering," (Jeremiah 25:15-29) and the meaning of baptism as death by drowning (Romans 6:3-4). He affirms that James and John will suffer greatly for their association with Jesus. Nevertheless, he refuses their request on the grounds that assigning such places is not his prerogative to give (which presumably belongs to his Father).

10:41–45. The anger of the other ten apostles at James and John provides the occasion for Jesus to redefine leadership as the service of others. He first contrasts this kind of leadership with the raw power they all experience from the Romans in their occupation of Palestine. Then he insists that in his movement, the leader must be the "slave of all." The usual situation was that a slave belonged to one master. The expression "slave of all" underlines Jesus' ideal of universal service toward others. Jesus presents himself as the best example of his teaching about servant leadership. He claims that as the Son of Man he has come to serve others to the point of giving his life as "a ransom for many" (see Isaiah 53). The term *ransom* (Greek, *lytron*) suggests that Jesus' death will have a sacrificial dimension, and will serve to bring about freedom from sin and death and then a new relationship with God.

10:46–52. Jesus' healing of blind Bartimaeus is really a dialogue of faith. Jericho is the last stop on the journey before his arrival at Jerusalem in 11:1. When Jesus is leaving Jericho,

Bartimaeus keeps shouting, "Jesus, Son of David, have mercy on me." The most prominent Son of David was Solomon, who in Jesus' time was revered as a magician and a healer. Impressed by Bartimaeus's persistence, Jesus summons him, asks what he wants, and learns that Bartimaeus hopes to see again. In response Jesus declares, "Your faith has made you well." The healing is immediate and complete, in contrast to the gradual healing that prefaced the journey in 8:22–26. The note that Bartimaeus "followed him on the way" indicates that he joined Jesus and his disciples on the road to Jerusalem.

For Reflection and Discussion

Why is it so hard to accept a suffering Messiah? What kind of heroes do we glorify today?

How do you understand the Transfiguration in 9:2–8? What did Moses represent to the Jewish people? What did Elijah represent?

How do you react to the disciples' growing confusion about Jesus? If you had been in their place, what would have bothered you most during this period of time, and why?

He sat down opposite the treasury, and watched the crowd putting money into the treasury. Many rich people put in large sums. A poor widow came and put in two small copper coins, which are worth a penny. Then he called his disciples and said to them, "Truly I tell you, this poor widow has put in more than all those who are contributing to the treasury. For all of them have contributed out of their abundance; but she out of her poverty has put in everything she had, all she had to live on."

—Mark 12:41–44

6

Jesus' Ministry in Jerusalem
Mark 11:1—13:37

It is to Mark 11—16 that we owe the idea of Holy Week:

- On Palm Sunday Jesus arrives in Jerusalem at the head of a solemn procession full of symbolic significance. On the next day he performs another symbolic action in the temple area.
- On the following days he enters into a series of debates or controversies with various Jewish groups in Jerusalem, and offers a long discourse about the events surrounding the full coming of God's kingdom.
- On Holy Thursday, after dining with his disciples, Jesus is arrested and tried by the Jewish leaders.
- On Good Friday he is condemned, executed, and buried.
- On Easter Sunday his tomb is found empty, and he is proclaimed to have been raised from the dead.

11:1–11. Jesus' entrance into Jerusalem is best understood as a prophetic demonstration and a symbolic action. The village of Bethany near the Mount of Olives will be Jesus' base during Holy Week (see 11:12; 14:3). There he arranges for the use of a young donkey on which he will ride into the city, thus fulfilling the prophecy of Zechariah 9:9: "your king comes to you . . . on a donkey." Also, according to Zechariah 14:4, the Mount of Olives will be the place where "the day of the LORD" will begin. As the procession enters the city, the crowd shouts words from Psalm 118:25–26 and interprets Jesus' arrival in terms of the coming of God's kingdom and of the Davidic Messiah: "Blessed is the coming kingdom of our ancestor David." After entering the temple compound and looking around, Jesus returns to Bethany.

11:12–25. Jesus' dealing with the fig tree is sandwiched around his cleansing of the temple. Both episodes are best understood as symbolic actions. The cursing of the fig tree appears to be an irrational action on Jesus' part, since (as Mark admits) Passover was "not the season for figs." The action is a foreshadowing, or a commentary, on the hostile reception that Jesus will receive in Jerusalem, and of the city's eventual destruction. At the very least, Jesus' cleansing of the temple is a criticism of the commercialism that has infected the operation of the sacrificial system there. Jesus defends his actions on the basis of a combination of Isaiah 56:7 and Jeremiah 7:11. Jesus' action gains the attention of the chief priests and scribes, who will be the leaders of the Jewish opposition to Jesus as the week's events unfold. Peter's observation about the withered fig tree becomes the occasion for a loosely related instruction about the power of prayer.

Controversies

11:27–33. The first in the series of five controversies concerns the authority of Jesus. It takes place on the third day of Holy Week and involves the chief priests, scribes, and elders. They want to know by what authority Jesus has been acting in his prophetic demonstrations and throughout his public ministry. Jesus answers them with another question, about John the Baptist's authority. This presents the opponents with a dilemma. If they say that John was from God, then they will have to explain why they did not accept him as a prophet. If they deny that John was from God, then they will lose support from those who admired John. Instead of answering Jesus' question, they simply say, "We do not know." Thus, Jesus outwits his opponents and avoids what could have been a danger to him and his followers.

12:1–12. The series of controversies is interrupted by the parable of the vineyard. The audience remains the same as in 11:27–33: the chief priests, scribes, and elders. The way in which the owner's actions are described in 12:1 evokes the parable of the vineyard in Isaiah 5:1–7. The owner, having gone away to another country, sends a series of slaves (the prophets) to collect his profits. However, the tenants in the vineyard abuse and even kill his messengers. Finally he sends his own son (Jesus?) on the grounds that he will be respected. But the son, too, is killed and even thrown outside the vineyard. His fate is expressed in terms of Psalm 118:22–23 as the rejected stone who becomes the cornerstone. The owner is said to come and destroy the tenants (but not the vineyard!) and to give the vineyard to others. What the parable prophesies is not the destruction of the vineyard (Israel) but rather a change in its leadership. And according to 12:12, the Jewish leaders perceive that the parable is about them.

12:13–17. The second controversy concerns paying taxes to the Romans. Here the questioners are Pharisees and Herodians (see 3:6). Their intent is hostile, and their question is, "Is it lawful to pay taxes to the emperor or not?" If Jesus says yes, the political insurgents will be angry with him. If he says no, then he will anger those who accept and support the Romans. Rather than give a direct answer, Jesus asks for a Roman coin with the emperor's image and inscription upon it. His point is that the questioners are already participating in the emperor's economic system, and so are answering their own question. Jesus' saying also suggests that they should be as serious and careful (indeed more so) in carrying out their obligations to God as they are to paying taxes to the emperor. Again Jesus outwits the opponents and avoids another dangerous situation.

12:18–27. In the debate about resurrection the questioners are Sadducees, the group that rejects the doctrine as not biblical. With their case about the woman who had seven husbands, they want to reduce the doctrine to absurdity on the basis of Deuteronomy 25:5–10. They most likely already know that Jesus sides with the Pharisees on this matter. In response Jesus claims that the Sadducees do not understand the nature of resurrected life ("[they] are like angels"). Then he brings forward the passages in Exodus 3 where God identifies himself as the God of Abraham, Isaac, and Jacob. The implication is that those patriarchs must be still alive, since God is the God of the living.

12:28–34. The fourth controversy concerns the greatest commandment in the Law of Moses. Here the questioner is a scribe, someone well versed in the Law and the Scriptures. Unlike the other debating partners, this scribe is not hostile and even agrees with Jesus' teaching. Jesus' answer consists of two biblical commandments: love of God (Deuteronomy 6:5) and love of neighbor (Leviticus 19:18). The scribe not only affirms Jesus' response but even takes it further, by declaring that keeping these commandments is more important than the sacrifices offered in the temple. In return Jesus declares that this scribe is "not far from the kingdom of God."

12:35–37. The final Jerusalem controversy is really a monologue about the proper interpretation of Psalm 110:1 ("the LORD says to my Lord") and the relationship between the Messiah and the Son of David. Here there are no opponents, and Jesus asks his own question. Jesus seizes on the double use of "Lord" understood as God addressing the newly anointed king, and notes that David (the alleged author of the psalm) calls the latter "my Lord." Jesus concludes that the Messiah must be even more important than the Son of David. The crowd takes delight in Jesus' argument.

12:38–44. Jesus contrasts the scribes and a poor widow, thus completely reversing the order of status in his Jewish society. He criticizes the scribes (paragons of intellectual and religious virtue and accomplishment) as ostentatious in their displays of piety while preying upon defenseless widows and swindling them out of their property. The poor widow (at the bottom of the social scale) can contribute only a few small coins to the temple treasury. Nevertheless, in Jesus' view, her integrity and sincerity raise her far above the scribes, and rich people in general, in the realm of piety and virtue.

The "Little Apocalypse"

Jesus' discourse in Mark 13 is often called the "Little Apocalypse," as opposed to the "Great Apocalypse" found in the book of Revelation. An apocalypse is a revelation about the future or about the heavenly realm.

- **13:1–4.** The setting of Jesus' discourse is the Mount of Olives, where "the day of the LORD" is to begin, according to Zechariah 14:4. On leaving the temple complex, some of the disciples marvel at the large stones and the huge buildings there. Jesus responds that they all will be demolished. When they move to the Mount of Olives, the first four disciples he called inquire about when this destruction will take place.
- **13:5–13.** In the first part of the discourse, Jesus describes the appearance of those who will try to impersonate him ("I am he!"), as well as wars, earthquakes, and famines as only "the beginning of the birth pangs." He goes on to warn that his followers can expect persecutions and family divisions.
- **13:14–23.** In the second part, Jesus deals with the "great tribulation" that will be triggered by the "desolating sacrilege" (both phrases come from the book of Daniel), and warns against being led astray by the appearance of false messiahs and false prophets.

- **13:24–27.** In the third part, using terms taken from various parts of the Old Testament, Jesus describes the cosmic portents that will lead up to the triumphant manifestation of the glorious Son of Man and the vindication of the "elect."
- **13:28–37.** In the fourth part, Jesus presents an exhortation consisting of parables and sayings, with some mixed messages ("this generation . . . no one knows"). Yet, he urges confidence in God's plan and constant vigilance as the divine plan unfolds and reaches its climax in the fullness of God's kingdom.

For Reflection and Discussion

What were the first actions Jesus took when he entered Jerusalem? What symbolism and meaning do you find in those actions?

Some of the controversies between Jesus and the religious authorities had to do with Jesus' authority (whether Jews should pay taxes to the Roman government, resurrection, and the greatest commandment from God). What was at stake for the Pharisees? What was at stake for Jesus? How might these issues have contributed to his death?

Why do you think Jesus went into such detail about the end times, in 13:1–37? Given Jesus' instructions to be vigilant, how might such watchfulness influence the way a Christian lives?

While they were eating, he took a loaf of bread, and after blessing it he broke it, gave it to them, and said, "Take; this is my body." Then he took a cup, and after giving thanks he gave it to them, and all of them drank from it. He said to them, "This is my blood of the covenant, which is poured out for many. Truly I tell you, I will never again drink of the fruit of the vine until that day when I drink it new in the kingdom of God."

—Mark 14:22–25

7

Jesus' Death and Resurrection in Jerusalem

Mark 14:1—16:20

The story of Jesus' suffering, death, and resurrection—the passion narrative—is the goal toward which the whole of Mark's Gospel has been pointing. The events take place at Passover, the spring festival celebrated by Jews as the memorial of their liberation from slavery in Egypt during Moses' time. As a pilgrimage festival, it attracted large crowds to Jerusalem and its temple. According to 14:2, the plotters against Jesus were afraid that any action against him might lead to a riot.

The Plot

14:1–11. In Mark's typical "sandwich" technique, the story of the plot is interrupted by Jesus' anointing by an unnamed woman during a meal at Bethany. Her action at the beginning of the passion narrative designates Jesus as "the Anointed One" (Messiah) and also foreshadows his death by alluding to the rituals surrounding his burial. The plotting resumes when the chief priests find a willing collaborator in Judas Iscariot, one of Jesus' twelve apostles. Their bribing Judas for his treachery contrasts with the woman's great generosity.

14:12–16. Mark designates Jesus' Last Supper as an official Passover meal. (John is more likely correct in placing it on the evening before the official Passover observance.) It's not clear whether Jesus' instructions to his disciples reflect arrangements already made or are meant as proof of his power of prophecy (as in 11:1–10).

14:17–31. The account of the Last Supper itself consists of Jesus' prophecies about Judas's treachery and Peter's denials, interrupted by the institution of the Eucharist. In prophesying Judas's betrayal, Jesus exhibits his foreknowledge while at the same time insisting on the moral responsibility of the betrayer. Likewise, his prophecy of Peter's denials shows that Jesus knows Peter better than Peter knows himself. In both cases there are references to biblical texts (Psalm 41:9 and Zechariah 13:7) that suggest that events are proceeding according to God's will as revealed in the Scriptures. Using the simple elements of bread and wine characteristic of festive Jewish meals, Jesus in 14:22–25 identifies the bread broken and passed around as "my body" and the cup of wine shared by all as "my blood of the covenant." He also connects this meal with the eternal banquet celebrated in the kingdom of God. Thus he invites his followers to share in his passion and death and also in his glory. He renews the covenant between God and his people sealed with the sprinkling of blood in Exodus 24:8, and he interprets his death in sacrificial terms and as having the effect of saving "many."

Jesus' Arrest

14:32–42. After the supper, Jesus and his disciples go out to the Mount of Olives (on the eastern slope of Jerusalem), to a garden called Gethsemane. Here Jesus must school himself to accept the cup of suffering that is before him. He takes along Peter, James, and John. He displays great emotion ("distressed and agitated . . . deeply grieved") in the spirit of the biblical lament psalms (see Psalms 42:6; 43:5). In his prayer he addresses God as "Abba, Father" and asks that God might take this cup of suffering from him. He finally accepts the suffering before him as being in accord with God's will. His heroic faithfulness contrasts with the weakness of his disciples. In the end, Jesus declares that his "hour" has come (the time of his passion, death, and resurrection) and that his betrayer and the other plotters are closing in on him.

14:43–52. Judas betrays Jesus in the garden. Since Passover was a pilgrimage feast, there would be many people moving about the city. For the arrest of Jesus to go smoothly, the plotters arranged for Judas to identify Jesus by giving him the ceremonial kiss that was customary for disciples to give their teacher and to greet him as "Rabbi" ("my exalted one"). The irony here is extreme. There is some resistance when an unnamed disciple cuts off the ear of the high priest's slave. By contrast, Jesus professes his own nonviolence and innocence. He insists that he is not a "bandit" (a term with political overtones like "insurgent" today), and that he has been teaching publicly without incident. But he accepts his arrest as being in accord with God's will as revealed in the Scriptures. And so the disciples' desertion of Jesus fulfills his prophecy in 14:27 based on Zechariah 13:7: "I will strike the shepherd, and the sheep

will be scattered." The flight of the young man in 14:51–52 provides a specific example of the betrayal of Jesus by one his own followers. (Who exactly the young man was remains a puzzle. Some
have suggested that it was the Evangelist himself.)

The Trials

**14:53–72. The trial of Jesus before the Jewish council fea-
tures another "sandwich" in which Peter's cowardice contrasts with Jesus' fidelity.** When Jesus is brought to the high
priest's house for a hearing, Peter follows at a distance. At the
trial two charges emerge: that Jesus threatened to destroy the
Jerusalem temple, and that he claims to be the Messiah and Son
of God. Jesus finally accepts publicly the titles of Messiah, Son
of God, and Son of Man—precisely at what seems to others the
lowest moment in his life. To the high priest and the other officials, however, this admission constitutes blasphemy. And so they
condemn him to death and abuse him. Meanwhile, Peter three
times denies being part of Jesus' movement and even knowing
him, thus fulfilling Jesus' prophecy in 14:30.

**15:1–20. Jesus undergoes a second "trial" before the
Roman prefect, or governor, Pontius Pilate.** After an early
morning consultation among the Jewish officials, they hand Jesus
over to Pilate. When Pilate asks whether he is the "King of the
Jews" (a Gentile translation of *Messiah*), Jesus gives an ambigu-
ous reply ("You say so"). When Pilate gives the crowd a choice
between releasing Jesus or Barabbas (a convicted insurgent), the
chief priests stir up the crowd to ask that Barabbas be released

and Jesus be crucified. According to Mark, Pilate relents, releases Barabbas, and has Jesus scourged in order to prepare him for execution by crucifixion—a public punishment inflicted on rebels and slaves. The mockery of Jesus by the soldiers plays off the rituals associated with emperors and kings: purple cloak, crown, greeting, kneeling, paying homage, and so on. The irony is that for Mark and his readers, Jesus really is the King of the Jews.

The Crucifixion

15:21–32. The place of crucifixion is Golgotha, outside the city walls. The time is 9:00 A.M. For the crucifixion, Simon of Cyrene is enlisted to carry the horizontal beam, presumably because Jesus is already too weak to do so. Jesus refuses the wine mixed with myrrh, intended to soften the pain. His garments are divided among the soldiers, thus fulfilling Psalm 22:18. The official charge is "King of the Jews"—that is, "Here is another would-be Jewish Messiah." His crucifixion is intended to deter others who might try to foment a rebellion against the Roman occupiers and their Jewish collaborators. This message is underlined by having Jesus crucified alongside two bandits (insurgents-terrorists). The mockery from passersby and from the chief priests and scribes recalls the two charges raised against Jesus during the Jewish trial: that he threatened to destroy the temple, and that he said he was the Messiah and Son of God. Even the bandits crucified along with him join in the mockery.

15:33–39. The death of Jesus takes place in darkness at 3:00 p.m. (see Amos 8:9–10). His last words are the first words of

Psalm 22: "My God, my God, why have you forsaken me?" A reading of the entire psalm shows that these are not the words of someone in despair. Rather, they are part of the process outlined in the biblical laments: address to God, complaints, professions of trust in God, petitions for help, and final vindication. Some bystanders think Jesus is calling on Elijah as the patron of the hopeless, and so he is offered sour wine. Mark describes the death of Jesus in a remarkably concise and cool way: "Then Jesus gave a loud cry and breathed his last." At the moment of his death the curtain of the temple is torn in two, most likely symbolizing the new way of relating to God brought about through Jesus' death and resurrection. The Gentile centurion overseeing Jesus' execution acknowledges, "Truly this man was God's Son!" This is the moment toward which the entire Gospel has been pointing from the start.

15:40–47. Only at this point, near the end of Mark's Gospel, do we learn about women disciples who have followed Jesus throughout his ministry and who witness his death and burial. The most prominent among the women is Mary Magdalene. She and some other women watch Jesus die. The man who takes charge of the body is Joseph of Arimathea. It's not clear if Mark regarded him as a disciple of Jesus. In accord with Deuteronomy 21:22–23, Joseph takes upon himself the task of seeing to Jesus' burial before the Sabbath begins. The burial is in Joseph's burial cave outside the city walls. From the interchange between Joseph and Pilate it is clear that Jesus is really dead. His corpse is wrapped in a shroud, and the cave opening is secured by rolling a large stone in front of it. Mary Magdalene and the other women see where he is buried.

The Resurrection

16:1–8. On Easter Sunday morning Mary Magdalene and her companions go to Jesus' tomb to complete the burial rituals. Their task is to perfume the corpse so that it might decompose over a year's time when the bones would then be gathered and placed in a stone container called an ossuary ("bone box"). To the women's great surprise, what they find is that the stone has been rolled away and the cave is empty. Inside the tomb they hear from a "young man" that Jesus has been raised ("he is not here"). He also tells them that the risen Jesus will meet up with the disciples in Galilee, just as he told them in 14:28. The women react with a mixture of fear and awe, and say nothing. The text of Mark's Gospel seems to break off here. His readers all knew about Jesus' resurrection. Perhaps the point was to send the readers back to the beginning again, and to make Jesus' story even more their own as they moved into the future.

The "shorter ending" of Mark's Gospel smoothes out the abrupt ending by explaining how the women reported to those around Peter, and how Jesus sent the apostles out to proclaim the good news. The language and style of this ending are quite different from the rest of Mark's Gospel.

16:9–20. The "longer ending" seems to have been a second-century summary, or compendium, of accounts of appearances of the risen Jesus in the other Gospels.

- the appearance to Mary Magdalene (Matthew 28:1–10; John 20:11–18)
- the appearance to the disciples on the road to Emmaus (Luke 24:13–35)

- the commissioning of the disciples (Matthew 28:16–20; Luke 24:44–49; John 20:19–23)
- the ascension of Jesus (Luke 24:50–53; Acts 1:1–11)

The addition of these two endings shows that some early Christian scribes were not satisfied with Mark's abrupt ending.

For Reflection and Discussion

How do you understand Jesus' struggle to accept the cup of suffering in the Gethsemane episode?

Read all of Psalm 22. How does this text help you to understand Jesus' passion, death, and resurrection?

What effect does the abrupt ending at Mark 16:8 have on you?

PART THREE

The Gospel of
Suffering in Context

Then the high priest tore his clothes and said, "Why do we still need witnesses? You have heard his blasphemy! What is your decision?" All of them condemned him as deserving death. Some began to spit on him, to blindfold him, and to strike him, saying to him, "Prophesy!" The guards also took him over and beat him.

—Mark 14:63–65

8

What and Why Did Jesus Suffer?

The two great questions of Mark's Gospel are, *What did Jesus suffer?* and *Why did Jesus suffer?* In this chapter I want to explore those two questions with reference not only to Mark's story of Jesus' suffering, death, and resurrection but also to the rest of his Gospel. I will approach the first question by looking at the story itself. The second and more difficult question calls for a theological analysis that follows Mark's own clues about why Jesus suffered.

What Did Jesus Suffer?

There is an old maxim (from Martin Kähler in 1892) found in New Testament study that Mark's Gospel is a passion narrative with a long introduction. I want to show that what Mark presents in the first thirteen chapters of his Gospel prepares for and leads into the mystery of the cross.

In the preceding chapters we have used narrative criticism to look at the whole Gospel; now I want to use that same study tool to focus on one topic: the suffering of Jesus. As we read the

Gospel story simply in light of the narrator, the characters, their interactions, and the plot line, we make one surprising discovery right away. Mark—the Evangelist of Jesus' suffering and the cross—places relatively little emphasis on the physical sufferings of Jesus. Rather, Jesus' physical sufferings and his death on the cross are the necessary consequences of something more fundamental: his being misunderstood and rejected by almost everyone throughout the Gospel story.

From the reader's perspective, it is puzzling and almost incredible that Jesus should be misunderstood and rejected. In the prologue (1:1–13) the narrator goes to great lengths to make sure that we know who Jesus is. The narrator of this Gospel lets us know from the beginning what God and the supernatural beings (demons and angels) know. We learn that Jesus' coming was foretold by the Jewish Scriptures and prophesied by John the Baptist (1:2–8), that he was declared by a voice from heaven as God's Son and Beloved Servant (1:9–11), that he overcame testing by Satan (1:12–13), and that in his preaching and activity the kingdom of God "has come near" (1:14–15). Mark the narrator knows all this. We readers come to know it also, thanks to Mark. But the other human characters in the story do *not* know it.

Rejection by the religious leaders

Mark's Gospel is the story of how Jesus was misunderstood and rejected. The inevitable outcome was the cross. This theme is raised first in the midst of Jesus' successes as a healer and a teacher at Capernaum (1:16—3:6). It comes out most clearly in the last verse of that section: "The Pharisees went out and immediately conspired with the Herodians against him, how to destroy him" (3:6). But it is signaled earlier in the block of five controversies, in which Jesus' pious and educated opponents (usually the Pharisees) object to

- his claim to forgive sins (2:5–10)
- his eating with tax collectors and sinners (2:16–17)
- his disciples' failure to fast (2:18)
- their doing "work" on the Sabbath (2:24)
- his healing on the Sabbath (3:2–4).

The opposition of the Pharisees as a group to Jesus continues through his ministry in Galilee and Jerusalem. In the passion narrative however, the Pharisees disappear and are replaced as Jesus' primary opponents by the chief priests, elders, and scribes.

Rejection by family members and hometown people

The misunderstanding and rejection of Jesus by his religious opponents are repeated by the reactions of his family. Jesus' family seems surprised and embarrassed by his success and the popular enthusiasm generated by it. They apparently believe the interpretation that "he has gone out of his mind" (3:21), and so they seek to restrain him. Their reaction in turn leads Jesus to redefine his family in spiritual terms: "Whoever does the will of God is my brother and sister and mother" (3:35). Sandwiched between these notices about Jesus' family is a debate between Jesus and the scribes from Jerusalem (3:22–30) concerning the source of his powers: Is it Satan or the Holy Spirit? The logic of

Jesus' response is that, if his power were from Satan, he would not be able to work against Satan's kingdom.

The scene at the synagogue in Jesus' hometown (6:1–6) adds to the misunderstanding and rejection. Like his family, the people of Jesus' hometown cannot understand the source of his teachings and his healing power. They think that they know all there is to know about Jesus because they know his occupation and his family. Thus they manifest the prejudice of familiarity: because they think they know so much about Jesus, they imagine that they know everything about him. In fact, they do not know what is really important about Jesus, what we know from the prologue, that Jesus is God's Son and Beloved Servant sent to proclaim God's kingdom. Thus the second phase of Jesus' Galilean ministry also ends on a note of misunderstanding and rejection.

Rejection by the disciples

Thus far in the plot, Jesus' disciples stand in contrast to the Pharisees and scribes, Jesus' family, and the people of his hometown. His own disciples start well but eventually misunderstand and reject Jesus. Recognizing that something is marvelously attractive about Jesus, the first four disciples respond without hesitation to Jesus' call to follow him (1:16–20). These four then become part of the group of twelve who are called "to be with him, and to be sent out to proclaim the message" (3:14). At the beginning of the third phase of Jesus' Galilean ministry, the Twelve are sent to do what Jesus did: to proclaim God's kingdom and to heal the sick (6:7–13). They witness and are part of not one but two multiplications of loaves and fishes (6:30–44; 8:1–10) as well as the scene of Jesus walking on the waters (6:47–52).

At this point one would expect the disciples to grow in their understanding and acceptance of Jesus. But in fact the opposite occurs. An ominous note is sounded after the first multiplication and the walking on the water: "for they did not understand about the loaves, but their hearts were hardened" (6:52). The depth of the disciples' misunderstanding is exposed by the passage that ends the third phase of Jesus' Galilean ministry (see Mark 8:17–21). Using a series of brutally direct questions, Jesus shows that the disciples do not yet understand. To come to real understanding they (and we) need to accompany Jesus on the way to Jerusalem and to the cross. Yet even then the disciples fail to understand and in fact grow more confused.

On the way to Jerusalem Jesus teaches his disciples (and us) about his identity (Christology) and about following him (discipleship). There are three predictions of his suffering and death (8:31; 9:31; 10:33–34). Each prediction is met with misunderstanding by Jesus' disciples. They fail to understand the wisdom of the cross, leadership as the service of the "least," and status in God's kingdom. Thus the distance between Jesus (and the readers) and his disciples grows. As readers we come to understand the mystery of the cross. Those closest to Jesus do not.

In the first part of Jesus' Jerusalem ministry the disciples' misunderstanding is not especially prominent. After an enthusiastic welcome by the crowds, Jesus enters into conflict with the leaders of his people again as in Galilee. These conflicts take the forms of controversies and the parable of the wicked tenants, which the leaders correctly perceive as being about themselves. The apocalyptic discourse, which is directed to the disciples, contains a foreshadowing of persecutions awaiting the followers of Jesus and a warning to be watchful always.

Mark 1—13 is indeed a long introduction to Jesus' passion; all the characters and plot lines come together in it:

- Jesus knows what awaits him.
- He accepts his fate, though not without some difficulty.
- The chief priests, elders, and scribes join forces with Pontius Pilate to put Jesus to death. The Jerusalem crowds turn from their Palm Sunday enthusiasm and call for Jesus to be crucified.
- Judas initiates the betrayal of Jesus.
  The rest of the Twelve desert him and flee.
- Jesus dies reciting the lament of the righteous sufferer (Psalm 22), which begins "My God, my God, why have you forsaken me?"

Women were the exception

There is one surprising exception to the almost complete misunderstanding and rejection of Jesus: the women. Before the passion narrative, one would hardly suspect that Jesus had women followers. Women show faith in Jesus and are healed. But they do not appear on the same level as—or even in the company of—the Twelve. Yet the woman who anoints Jesus at Bethany (14:3–9) sees what the Twelve fail to see: Jesus is the Messiah (the "anointed one"); this is the decisive moment in salvation history; and Jesus' death is part of God's good news ("gospel"). The women at the scene of the cross (15:40–41) are finally introduced as having followed Jesus and provided for him in Galilee, and as having come up with him to Jerusalem. The women see Jesus die, ascertain where he is buried, and discover the tomb empty on Easter morning. The women are the embodiment of continuity and fidelity in the story of Jesus' suffering and death.

So we see, throughout this Gospel, the nature of Jesus' suffering: Almost everyone misunderstands and rejects him, and his passion and death are the culmination of misunderstanding and rejection. At the beginning of the story, those whom Jesus calls to be with him and to share his ministry are exceptions. But as the events unfold they, too, misunderstand Jesus, and by deserting him in effect reject him—only to accept him as their risen Lord after Easter (see 14:28; 16:7). At the end of the story, certain women emerge as truly faithful followers who witness Jesus' final sufferings and death, and discover that his tomb is indeed empty.

Why Did Jesus Suffer?

What Jesus suffered is relatively clear. Why he suffered is a more difficult topic. Mark's Gospel is a story about Jesus, not a catechism or theological treatise. There is no extensive or systematic treatment of this topic from Mark—nor should we expect one. What we do have are clues or hints in the course of the story. These clues can be taken as part of a larger picture in working out a New Testament or biblical theology of suffering. Or they can be used as starting points for theological reflections on suffering.

My goal here is more modest. I want simply to identify Mark's clues. I discern three major reasons given by Mark for why Jesus suffers.

- The cross is God's will.
- Jesus' suffering and death are "for us."
- Jesus provides an example for suffering people.

God's will

We find several indications that the cross is God's will. The first passion prediction (8:31) suggests divine necessity: "The Son of Man must undergo great suffering." The title of the Gospel according to most manuscripts identifies Jesus as the Son of God. Only at the moment of Jesus' death does a human being identify Jesus in this way—then a Gentile centurion proclaims, "Truly this man was God's Son!" (15:39). As we have seen, the whole narrative leads up to this confession. The divine necessity is underscored by the many allusions to Old Testament texts, especially to Psalm 22, the psalm of the righteous sufferer (see Mark 15:24 = Psalm 22:18; Mark 15:29 = Psalm 22:7; Mark 15:34 = Psalm 22:1).

Mark apparently regarded Jesus' suffering as the paradoxical wisdom of God, much as Paul did in 1 Corinthians 1—4: "we proclaim Christ crucified, a stumbling block to Jews and foolishness to Gentiles (1:23), . . . for the wisdom of this world is foolishness with God" (3:19). Yet in Mark's Gospel Jesus accepts the cross only after struggle. This struggle is best described in the episode of Jesus' prayer at Gethsemane (14:32–42). As Jesus accepts his fate already foreseen in the immediately preceding episodes, he as the righteous sufferer of the biblical tradition struggles to accept the cup of suffering (see Jeremiah 49:12; Ezekiel 23:31–34). The pivotal saying is Mark 14:36: "He said, 'Abba, Father, for you all things are possible; remove this cup from me; yet, not what I want, but what you want.'"

We need not take Mark 14:36 or Jesus' words from the cross (15:34 = Psalm 22:1) as indicating final despair on Jesus' part. Nor should we dismiss them as mere literary imagination or biblical quotation. In the Bible there is a great deal of complaint about suffering. Indeed, the largest formal category in the book of Psalms is the lament. And Job, the Prophets, and Lamentations are full of laments by people in the midst of suffering. There is no real contradiction in the biblical tradition between accepting suffering as God's will and complaining about the reality of suffering. By his statement in Mark 14:36 Jesus affirms the omnipotence of God, prays that the cup of suffering might be removed, and in the end accepts the cross as being God's will for him. Thus he stands within the biblical tradition of lament in the midst of suffering.

Vicarious suffering

From the church's early times, Christians believed that Jesus' suffering and death had significance for us and for our sins. This interpretation existed before the time of Paul, and when Paul was writing in the fifties of the first century, he took it for granted and embraced it as his own (see Romans 3:25–26; 1 Corinthians 11:24; 15:3). Paul himself used similar expressions in his letters (see Romans 5:6; 14:15; 2 Corinthians 5:14, 21; Galatians 1:4; 3:13). All these phrases presuppose that Christ as God's Servant

suffered and died on our behalf, and thus made available to all—
Jews and Gentiles alike—justification, access to God, salvation,
and so forth. The "us" in these writings refers not merely to isolated individuals but rather to the collective that includes all who
are "in Christ." And being "in Christ" means sharing in Jesus'
suffering and death (see Romans 6:1–11; 2 Corinthians 1:3–7;
4:10; Philippians 3:10–11).

Because Mark was writing the story of Jesus' public ministry
and death, we should not expect a theological exposition of Jesus'
suffering and death "for us." However, there are indications that
Mark shared this early Christian understanding of Jesus' death.
The most striking clue is Mark 10:45: "For the Son of Man came
not to be served but to serve, and to give his life a ransom for
many." To give one's life suggests a voluntary surrender of one's
life or martyrdom (see 1 Maccabees 2:50; 6:44). The word *ransom* (*lytron* in Greek) conveys the notion of deliverance by purchase on behalf of captives, slaves, or criminals. The expression
"for many" echoes what is said about God's Suffering Servant in
Isaiah 53:11–12. The whole saying views Jesus' death as bringing
about a deliverance that could not have been accomplished for
"the many" by their own means.

Another important saying regarding Jesus' suffering and death
"for us" occurs in the Last Supper account: "This is my blood of the
covenant, which is poured out for many" (Mark 14:24). The "blood
of the covenant" alludes to when Moses sealed the Sinai covenant by
sprinkling the blood of sacrificial animals upon Israel (see Exodus
24:8). The "poured out for many" refers (as in Mark 10:45) to the
Suffering Servant of Isaiah 53:11–12. These two biblical allusions

reflect the early Christian interpretation of viewing Jesus' death as a sacrifice with significance and effects for others.

According to Mark, Jesus' suffering and death "for us" have eschatological and cosmic dimensions. Even before his public ministry Jesus withstands Satan's testing. In his public activity (especially his exorcisms and healings) Jesus shows that Satan's power is being broken. At Jesus' death, darkness covers the land and the curtain of the temple is torn in two. Jesus' talk about end-times makes it clear that the fullness of God's kingdom remains future. Nevertheless, in and through Jesus' ministry and particularly through his suffering and death, God's kingdom is made present—it is both inaugurated and anticipated.

Example for us

Mark portrays Jesus as a unique figure—as the Son of God whose suffering and death brought about redemption "for us." But by contrasting Jesus with Israel's leaders, his family and fellow Nazarenes, and his disciples, Mark places upon Jesus special significance. The suffering Christ appears as an example and a source of encouragement to a community living in an atmosphere of hostility and perhaps actual persecution. We don't need to know whether Mark's community was located in Rome or the East (Galilee, Syria, Alexandria?), and whether it was anticipating, undergoing, or looking back on persecution. It is enough to note what is, in fact, the scholarly consensus: Mark wrote for a community in which suffering was a reality.

Mark's Jesus shows compassion to those who suffer. In his many healings and exorcisms, he not only alleviates the physical sufferings of others but also treats them with genuine emotion and pity (see 1:41; 3:5; 10:14). Also, there are hints that some Christians so focused on Jesus' powers as a healer that they neglected the challenge of the cross. Mark wished to show such persons that there is no adequate understanding of Jesus apart from the cross. And so everything in Mark's Gospel leads up to and climaxes in the story of Jesus' passion and death. His miracles and his teachings cannot be separated from the cross.

Finally, Jesus invites those who follow him along the way to "deny themselves and take up their cross" (8:34). He promises them that in their willingness to "lose their life for my sake, and for the sake of the gospel" they will save it (8:35). When we follow Jesus faithfully, we will suffer. Yet persecution and suffering do not mean the defeat of the Christian movement, any more than they meant the end of Jesus. Just as Jesus accepted the cross as the fate of the suffering righteous one and as God's will revealed in the Scriptures, so Jesus' followers are encouraged to deal with suffering according to his good example and to recognize that God is present even (and especially) in the mystery of suffering as symbolized by the cross.

Mark's Gospel is the story of an innocent person who was misunderstood and treated unjustly. It is the story of someone who foresaw the suffering ahead, struggled with it, and accepted it as God's will for him. According to Mark, the essence of being Jesus' disciple is being with Jesus. Mark's Gospel challenges us to remain with Jesus even (and especially) in his suffering and death, and there find God. (In this chapter I have drawn some material from my article "What and Why Did Jesus Suffer according to Mark," *Chicago Studies* 34 [1995], 32–41.)

For Reflection and Discussion

Why do you think Mark gives relatively little attention to the physical sufferings of Jesus?

What aspect of Jesus' suffering do you think was most difficult, and why?

Which theological explanation for why Jesus suffered do you find most satisfactory (and least satisfactory)?

9

Biblical Perspectives on Suffering

Why me? This question arises spontaneously when we suffer, whether the occasion is trivial (a bad cold, an argument) or serious (a cancer diagnosis or damage from a flood). As humans, we have a deep desire to find a reason for our suffering and to discover some meaning in it.

The Bible provides several answers to the question, Why me? Suffering may be just punishment for foolish or sinful behavior. Suffering may be a discipline, an experience from which we can learn and become better persons. Suffering may be for the benefit of others. Or suffering may be mysterious at best or meaningless at worst. For those in the midst of suffering and searching for meaning, the Bible's lament psalms can be a precious resource in building a community of sufferers.

Just Punishment

The question "Why me?" is often accompanied by another question, "What did I do wrong?" Deep in the human psyche is the notion that suffering is the result of foolish or sinful behavior. And it often is! How many persons have been killed by drunk drivers? How many have shortened their own lives by excessive smoking?

People get what they deserve in life—or so says the law of retribution. The principle that the just are rewarded and the wicked are punished is all over the Bible. For example, "The integrity of the upright guides them, but the crookedness of the treacherous destroys them" (Proverbs 11:3). In Deuteronomy 30:15–20, Moses places before Israel a choice. To choose life means to obey God's commandments and so to enjoy happiness and prosperity, whereas turning from God will lead to suffering and death. The story of Adam and Eve in Genesis 3 suggests that the suffering and death that all humans experience are the consequences of the "original sin."

Yet the law of retribution does not always seem to apply. The sage known as Ecclesiastes expresses a skepticism founded on his wide experience: "There are righteous people who perish in their righteousness, and there are wicked people who prolong their life in their evildoing" (Ecclesiastes 7:15). And on several occasions (see Luke 13:1–5 and John 9:3) Jesus denies that sin is the only explanation for suffering.

Divine Discipline

Overcoming adversity is an element in many "success" stories: the Olympic champion runner who had polio as a child (Wilma Rudolph), stutterers who became great public speakers (Winston Churchill and James Earl Jones), or the celebrated writer who toiled in obscurity for many years (J. K. Rowling, the author of the Harry Potter book series). Such persons often look back on their sufferings and interpret them as learning experiences that gave them extraordinary desire and focus.

The theme of suffering as a discipline from God is prominent in late Old Testament writings. The wisdom teacher Ben Sira warns his prospective students: "My child, when you come to serve the Lord, prepare yourself for testing" (Sirach 2:1). He makes willingness to accept discipline into a condition for making progress in pursuing wisdom: "If you are willing, my child, you can be disciplined, and if you apply yourself you will become clever" (6:32). The author of 2 Maccabees explains the suffering endured by faithful Jews in the second century B.C. as a sign of God's mercy and care for them: "Although he disciplines us with calamities, he does not forsake his own people" (6:16).

The letter to the Hebrews is a long meditation on the meaning of Jesus' suffering and death "for us." Its exhortation in chapter 12 about suffering as a discipline from God takes as its starting point the sufferings of Jesus, "the pioneer and perfecter of our faith" (Hebrews 12:2), who endured a shameful death on the cross and so entered into glory at God's right hand. A quotation from Proverbs 3:11–12 ("the Lord disciplines those whom he loves") leads into a reflection on the discipline that loving parents impose upon their children. If we respect and love our parents for having disciplined us when we were children, then we should respect and love our heavenly Father when "he disciplines us for our good, in order that we may share his holiness" (Hebrews 12:10). The authors of Proverbs and Hebrews assume that the suffering will be temporary and will make us better persons, and that this kind of suffering can have an educative value in testing our character and helping us to understand better the ways of God. And sometimes it does.

Benefit for Others

When athletes sacrifice themselves and their own glory for the good of their team, they are praised and admired. When firefighters risk their lives to save others, they are hailed as heroes; and those who perish are said to "have not died in vain." When Martin Luther King Jr. was killed for proclaiming the gospel of justice and freedom, his witness had (and has) significance for all Americans. At least in certain circumstances we can understand the redemptive value of suffering; that is, the idea that the suffering of one person (or group) may benefit many others.

The most important Old Testament figure who suffers for others is the Suffering Servant of Isaiah 40—55. Whoever the Servant may have been in the sixth century B.C., he is portrayed in Isaiah 52:13—53:12 as someone whose suffering had a purpose and a positive effect for others. As a consequence of the Servant's suffering, the sins of God's people were wiped away so that they could return from exile in Babylon. His suffering is described as a sacrifice for sins: "But he was wounded for our transgressions, crushed for our iniquities; upon him was the punishment that made us whole, and by his bruises we are healed" (Isaiah 53:5). The Servant in turn becomes the model for the suffering righteous person of Wisdom 2—3, the Maccabean martyrs (2 Maccabees 6—7), and Jesus, the Servant of God.

As discussed earlier, Mark's Gospel, which is sometimes called the Gospel of Suffering, interprets Jesus' life and death in terms of service and vicarious suffering: "For the Son of Man came not to be served but to serve, and to give his life as a ransom for many" (10:45). During his ministry of teaching and healing in Galilee, Jesus attracts misunderstanding and opposition from Pharisees and Herodians, the people of Nazareth, and his own disciples. On the way to Jerusalem he predicts his death and resurrection three times, and each time he is misunderstood by his disciples. In Jerusalem the chief priests, scribes, and elders conspire to hand him over for execution to Pontius Pilate, the Roman prefect. Jesus' identity as Messiah, Son of God, and Son of Man becomes clear only at the moment when he is sentenced to suffer and die.

The earliest confessions of Christian faith (1 Corinthians 11:24; 15:3; Romans 3:25–26) proclaimed Jesus' suffering and death as "for us" and "for our sins," thus echoing Isaiah 53. Paul himself often used similar formulas. These creedal summaries affirm that Jesus suffered and died as God's Servant on our behalf, and so made available to all people a new relationship with God. His suffering is full of meaning.

According to Paul, believers can participate in Jesus' suffering and death as well as in his resurrection: "I want to know Christ . . . and the sharing of his sufferings by becoming like him in his death, if somehow I may attain the resurrection from the dead" (Philippians 3:10–11; see 2 Corinthians 1:3–7; 4:10). The Christian life is total identification with Jesus and involves a kind of Christ mysticism.

What about Colossians 1:24? There Paul says: "I am now rejoicing in my sufferings for your sake, and in my flesh I am completing what is lacking in Christ's afflictions." This cannot mean that there is something deficient in the reconciliation brought about by Christ (see Colossians 1:19–20). Rather, the idea seems to be that Paul's sufferings (and ours too) on behalf of other Christians may shorten the time before God's kingdom comes in its fullness (see Mark 13:20).

Mystery

When Cardinal Basil Hume of Great Britain was visiting a refugee camp in Ethiopia during a terrible famine some years ago, a reporter asked him why God allowed this catastrophe to happen. He replied, "I have no idea." There are many cases of human suffering where the usual answers—just punishment, divine discipline, or benefit for others—do not work. The case of Job is one.

Job is introduced as "blameless and upright, one who feared God and turned away from evil" (Job 1:1). When first deprived of his possessions and health, Job remained patient and trusting in God (1:21; 2:10). However, in chapter 3 Job lets out a howl and bewails his fate: "Why did I not die at birth?" (3:11).

So begins a long conversation (Job 4—37) between Job and his "friends" about the law of retribution and theodicy (God's justice). Three propositions are debated endlessly: God is all powerful; God is just; and the righteous are rewarded and the wicked are punished. Job's friends reason that since he is suffering, he must have sinned, because God is both omnipotent and just. Job, however, complains that God is not just. They all confront the mystery of innocent suffering (as Jesus does in Gethsemane) and do not know how to resolve it.

God's speeches from the whirlwind (Job 38—41) provide a change of perspective rather than an answer. God invites Job (and us) to view creation from God's perspective and to recognize how limited our human perspective is. There are areas that we cannot see or know, much less control. God's "answer" is that sometimes (as in Job's case) suffering is a mystery beyond human comprehension and what is needed are humility and acceptance in the face of mystery (see 42:1–6).

The mystery of suffering is the background for apocalypses like Daniel and Revelation and for much New Testament theology. Apocalyptic literature is crisis literature, generally emanating from suffering people. It defers the resolution of the mystery of innocent suffering to the Last Judgment. Then all creation will acknowledge the omnipotence and justice of God, and the righteous will be vindicated and the wicked punished. Christians believe that with Jesus' resurrection the end-time has already begun and God's kingdom is among us. And yet evil and death are at work in our world. Until the Last Judgment we experience the mystery of innocent suffering in our lives and try to confront it with hope and patient endurance.

A Community of Sufferers

Suffering is a universal human experience. Yet when we suffer, we often feel isolated and alienated. The Old Testament lament psalms can help suffering persons to break out of their loneliness. Psalm 3 is a good example of a lament. It begins with an address to God: "O LORD." Next there is a complaint: "Many are rising against me." Then there is a confession of faith in God ("you, O LORD, are a shield around me") and a profession of trust ("I lie down and sleep; . . . I am not afraid"). Next there is a petition: "Rise up, O LORD! Deliver me, O my God!" Finally there is a kind of thanksgiving: "Deliverance belongs to the LORD; may your blessing be on your people!"

The laments constitute about one-third of Old Testament Psalms (3, 5, 6, 7, 13, 17, 22, 25, 26, 27, 28, etc.). According to Matthew 27:46 and Mark 15:34, Jesus' last words were the first words from the lament known as Psalm 22: "My God, my God, why have you forsaken me?" To get the full meaning of Jesus' last words in those Gospels, it is necessary to read the whole psalm, which ends on a note of vindication and celebration.

The biblical laments can help sufferers recognize that they are not alone but stand in a long tradition of suffering people. These psalms allow sufferers to address God directly, to shake off their personal and religious inhibitions, and to express their feelings of pain, fear, and confusion. Also, they can help sufferers articulate the questions their suffering raises: Why am I suffering? Does it have any meaning? Where is God? How will things come out?

The Psalms of lament are part of our biblical heritage. Once used in liturgical celebrations at the Jerusalem temple, they are now embedded in a tradition that links millions of people all over the world. They remind us that those who suffer are honored members of our community of faith. The laments may be the Bible's most important contribution to the issue of suffering and meaning. They say: You are not alone; many have gone before you; it is all right to complain; it is all right to be angry, even with God; God is still there in your suffering; and there is always hope because "deliverance belongs to the LORD" (Psalm 3:8). (In this chapter I have drawn some material from my article "Why Me? Suffering and Meaning," in *Scripture from Scratch* [August 2002], 1–4.)

For Reflection and Discussion

Recall one of your own experiences of suffering. What was the occasion, and how did you react? How might the biblical materials have illumined that experience?

Where is God in human suffering? Does suffering call God's existence into question? What responsibility do we have to alleviate or overcome the causes of suffering?

In what sense is the church a "community of fellow sufferers"? What are the implications for the church of having Christ's suffering, death, and resurrection as its foundational event? What responsibilities does the church have toward those who suffer?

PART FOUR

Mark's Gospel in Christian Life

10

Biblical Variations on the Theme of Suffering

Suffering is a major theme in Mark's Gospel and in the Bible as a whole. During the Year B in the Sunday Lectionary cycle (2012, 2015, 2018, 2021, 2024, etc.), the selections from Mark's Gospel along with the accompanying readings often provide an opportunity to reflect on various aspects of Jesus' suffering and our own. The five meditations that follow are slightly retouched versions of my essays that first appeared in "The Word" column in *America* magazine in 2006. They illustrate some of the contributions that Mark makes in the library that is the Bible. They focus especially on the theme of suffering, and place it in the contexts of Christ's suffering, death, and resurrection and of the Christian life.

The Dangerous Memory of Jesus

Palm Sunday of the Lord's Passion (B)

Readings: Mark 11:1–10; Isaiah 50:4–7; Psalm 22:8–9, 17–20, 23–24; Philippians 2:6–11; Mark 14:1—15:47

> He humbled himself and became obedient to the
> point of death—even death on a cross.
>
> —Philippians 2:8

Jesus' suffering and death are important parts of our collective memory as Christians. For almost two thousand years Christians have gathered during Holy Week to retell the story of Jesus' passion and death. It is not the story of a mythical or fictional character. Rather, it is the story of a real historical person, Jesus of Nazareth, who was arrested, condemned, tortured, and executed in Jerusalem under Pontius Pilate. The readings for Palm-Passion Sunday can enrich and keep alive what theologian J. B. Metz calls the dangerous memory of Jesus.

The Gospel of Mark provides the framework of Holy Week. The week begins with Jesus' entrance into Jerusalem (11:1–10), at the end of his long journey with his disciples from northern Galilee. Mark's account of Palm Sunday introduces some themes that will be prominent in the larger story: Jesus knowingly and willingly embraces his fate; he is not only a humble Messiah but even a suffering Messiah; and he acts in accord with God's will as revealed in the Scriptures.

The readings for the Mass are among the richest texts in the Christian Bible. The passage from Isaiah 50 is one of the so-called servant songs. While the precise historical identity of the servant (the prophet himself, the king of Judah in exile, another leader in the exile community, the community itself, or Israel as a collective?) remains mysterious, it is clear that early Christians found in this figure a foretelling or anticipation of Jesus. The servant of Isaiah 50 is a poet-prophet like Jesus who endures mockery and physical harm in carrying out his divinely appointed mission. Despite his sufferings, he remains true to his calling out of the conviction that "the Lord God is my help."

Today's responsorial psalm is made up of verses from Psalm 22, one of the lament psalms. The first words in this psalm ("My God, my God, why have you forsaken me?") are the last words of Jesus according to Mark (15:34). However, they are not words of despair or disappointment. It is important to read the whole psalm, all thirty-one verses, and to take account of the literary conventions of the laments. After a direct address ("my God"), there are alternating sections of complaints about the speaker's present sufferings and affirmations of his trust in God. Then following a plea for God's help, there are ten verses that invite us to celebrate the speaker's restoration and vindication by God. Early Christians found in this lament psalm not only the prophecy of Jesus' passion and death but also a foreshadowing of his vindication in the resurrection.

The reading from Paul's letter to the Philippians (2:6–11) is generally regarded as an early Christian hymn that celebrates the abasement and exaltation of Jesus Christ. The first stanza recounts the incarnation and the passion and death of Jesus the Servant of God. By taking on our humanity, Jesus "emptied" himself of the privileges of divinity and embraced the most difficult aspects of human existence—suffering and death. The second stanza celebrates the resurrection and exaltation of Jesus the Servant, and all creation joins in proclaiming him as "Lord." All of these texts help us remember the suffering of Jesus, while reminding us that in his case, suffering and death did not have the last word.

Mark's Gospel is often described as a passion narrative with a long introduction, since the passion story (14:1—15:47) is so climactic and important in its overall plan. According to Mark, Jesus was a wise teacher and a powerful healer and miracle worker. He acts out of divine authority, and what he says and does constitute the inauguration or presence of God's kingdom. However, Mark insists that Jesus' identity as teacher and miracle worker can be properly understood only in light of the mystery of the cross. Among the themes running through Mark's story of Holy Week, the three mentioned above in connection with the Palm Sunday account are especially prominent: Jesus knowingly and willingly goes to his death; he is a humble and suffering Messiah; and all proceeds according to God's will as revealed to us in the Scriptures.

In the phrase made popular in theological circles by J. B. Metz, the story of Jesus' passion and death constitutes a "dangerous memory." His memory challenges many of the assumptions about life, happiness, and success that most people today hold dear. His memory confronts us with the terrible realities of misunderstanding, injustice, and innocent suffering. His memory shows us that even the Son of God had to struggle to accept God's will made manifest in the grim reality of the cross. And his memory places before us the surprising possibility that God can and does accomplish great and wonderful things even in the midst of terrible suffering. The memory that we keep alive during Holy Week is indeed a dangerous memory.

Praying with Scripture

What does it mean to call Jesus the "Servant of God"? What implications might this have for your Christian life?

Read the whole text of Psalm 22. In what respects is this psalm appropriate as the last words of Jesus?

What elements in Mark's passion narrative do you find especially challenging or "dangerous"?

Accepting and Alleviating Suffering
Twenty-Fourth Sunday in Ordinary Time (B)

Readings: Isaiah 50:5–9; Psalm 116:1–6, 8–9; James 2:14–18; Mark 8:27–35

> "If any want to become my followers, let them deny themselves and take up their cross and follow me."
> —Mark 8:34

In approaching the mystery of suffering, the Christian Bible puts forward Jesus as an example of faithfulness, a compassionate companion, and a model of hope. In many respects Jesus follows the pattern set by the Servant of the Lord in Isaiah 40—55. The Bible also challenges us to alleviate the sufferings of others, where possible.

Today's Old Testament reading from one of the four Servant songs in Isaiah describes the physical sufferings of God's Servant in gruesome detail. His back was scourged, his beard pulled out and his face spat upon. Before his trials he was not rebellious.

During and after them, he remained faithful to God and his mission, fully confident that in God he had a champion and a vindicator. The Servant remained faithful to God not so much out of personal courage or physical strength but because God had been faithful to him. He accepted his sufferings because he believed that God was with him and for him.

The Servant song from Isaiah 50 is paired with Mark 8:27–35, in which Peter's confession of Jesus as the Messiah is followed by Jesus' first prediction of his passion, death, and resurrection, and his challenge to take up the cross and follow him. The Servant passage provides background for the revelation of Jesus as the suffering Messiah. The reading from Mark 8 begins a series of seven Sunday Gospel readings from Mark's account of the journey of Jesus and his disciples from northern Galilee to Jerusalem. Along the way Jesus gives instructions about his identity and what it means to follow him.

Peter correctly identifies Jesus as "the Christ" or the Messiah. Where Peter is incorrect, it seems, concerns the kind of Messiah that Jesus is. Along with some of his Jewish contemporaries, Peter apparently imagines that Jesus will be a powerful Son of David who will be a military hero, wise ruler, and just judge for Israel all in one. (See *Psalms of Solomon* 17 for an example of such expectations.) What Peter (and we) had to learn was that Jesus came to be a suffering Messiah, one who cannot be understood properly apart from the mystery of the cross.

It is important to note that Jesus does not reject Peter's identification of him as the Messiah. What he does reject is the kind of ideas and expectations associated with the title in some circles. The real Messiah (Jesus) will have to suffer and die before his resurrection. Like the Servant, Jesus accepts suffering as part of his mission and out of fidelity toward the one whom he calls Father.

Jesus goes on to warn prospective followers that discipleship may involve their suffering, too. He challenges them to deny themselves, take up the cross, and follow him. The suffering Messiah invites his disciples to share in his suffering. But he also promises that in their sufferings they can and will find life and true freedom. Jesus foresaw that suffering would come his way, and he accepted and embraced it as God's will for him and as a benefit for others (for us and for our sins). His example provides a challenge for us all to accept the mystery of the cross when our turn comes to follow the Suffering Servant and Suffering Messiah.

The reading from James 2 reminds us that suffering is not only something to be accepted but also something to be alleviated. Suffering is not good in itself. And James, the master of practical spirituality, reminds us that our faith must express itself in our deeds and insists that (where possible) we have an obligation to alleviate suffering. Some interpreters have seen in this text a critique of Paul's doctrine of justification by faith or (more likely) of an extreme version of it that failed to grasp Paul's ethical ideal of "faith working through love" (Galatians 5:6).

James asks us to imagine a situation in which a poor person appears who does not have enough to wear or to eat. He insists that it is not enough to display a pleasant manner and to convey good wishes. He suggests that words like "Go in peace; keep warm and eat your fill" are really only a brush-off. Rather, James contends, we as Christians are obliged to meet the material needs of poor persons and to alleviate their sufferings. Otherwise, our faith is all talk and no action. As James notes, "Faith, by itself, if it has no works, is dead." The practical Christianity promoted by James insists that we must respond concretely to the needs and sufferings of our fellow humans.

Whether the challenge before us is to accept suffering or to alleviate suffering, we have wise and helpful teachings in today's biblical texts. And we have the example of Jesus the faithful, compassionate, and hopeful Servant of God and suffering Messiah.

Praying with Scripture

What are the similarities between the Suffering Servant and Jesus? What are some differences?

What elements in Jesus' approach to suffering are most helpful to you as you undergo suffering? What are less helpful?

What have you found to be practical and effective ways of alleviating the suffering of others?

Images of Servant Leadership
Twenty-Ninth Sunday in Ordinary Time (B)

Readings: Isaiah 53:10–11; Psalm 33:4–5, 18–20, 22; Hebrews 4:14–16; Mark 10:35–45

> For the Son of Man came not to be served but to serve, and to give his life a ransom for many.
>
> —Mark 10:45

As political campaigns draw near to election days, we hear much talk about leadership. While we tend to know it when we see it, leadership is hard to define and does not seem to follow one pattern or formula. Today's Scripture readings describe leadership as the service of others and portray Jesus as the best example of it. A series of images from Mark 10 and Hebrews 4 can help us grasp Jesus' noble and paradoxical notion of servant leadership.

In Scripture, the terms *cup* and *baptism* are sometimes images of suffering. To drink the cup is to accept the reality of suffering and to do God's will in the midst of it, as Jesus did in Gethsemane. To undergo a baptism is to be immersed in water and suffer a kind of drowning. The point that Jesus makes to James and John in Mark 10:38–39 is that those who follow the way of Jesus and seek to imitate his example of servant leadership must be willing even to suffer for others.

The images of leaders making their authority felt, and "lording" it over others stand in contrast to the leadership style of Jesus. Too often in our world, leadership involves a battle of wills and it means exercising force over others and making others conform to the leader's will. This prevalent pattern is far from Jesus' ideal of servant leadership.

To be "the slave of all" appears at first glance to be the opposite of being a leader. Slavery was an accepted institution in the Roman Empire and an integral part of the economic and social fabric of Greco-Roman society. To speak of a slave was not unusual. But to describe anyone as "the slave of all" made no sense. A slave could have only one master. How could anyone be the slave of all, and how could such a person be a leader? Nevertheless, Jesus, as a master of paradox in word and deed, brings these two concepts together in his concept of servant leadership.

The image of a "ransom" evokes the practice of buying someone out of slavery or kidnapping. When someone is enslaved or kidnapped, paying a ransom can sometimes get that person back to safety and freedom. The image suggests that Jesus' death on the cross was a kind of redemption or ransom that enabled us to gain freedom from sin and death and to share the intimate relationship that he enjoyed with his heavenly Father. The idea is rooted in the Servant of the Lord described in Isaiah 53:11: "The righteous one, my servant, shall make many righteous." The goal of Jesus' life and death was not power over others but rather the service of others. As the one who came not to be served but to serve, Jesus provides the pattern and the measure of his own ideal of servant leadership.

To express the effects of Jesus' servant leadership, the author of Hebrews uses the images of "sacrifice" and "priest." Like other early Christians, he understood Jesus' death on the cross to be an atoning sacrifice for sins. Because Jesus freely and willingly went to his death for us, the author of Hebrews reasons that Jesus can therefore be regarded as a priest (since priests customarily offered sacrifices). He further argues that unlike the Jewish high priests who offered sacrifices yearly on the Day of Atonement, Jesus— who offered himself once for all as the perfect sacrifice for sins— can be called the great High Priest.

Like other New Testament writers, the author of Hebrews interpreted the passion, death, resurrection, and exaltation of Jesus as one great comprehensive event—what we know as the paschal mystery. In describing the last element, he uses the image of Jesus passing through the heavens to return to his Father. Because of the paschal mystery, the author of Hebrews can encourage his confused and weary audience to hold fast to their confession of faith. His point is this: The one truly effective sacrifice for sins has been offered in Jesus' death on the cross. Christ, the great High Priest, has done his saving work, and the victory has been won once and for all. We do not have to do what the Jewish high priests did yearly on the Day of Atonement, because what Jesus did is more than sufficient. This message is the author's word of consolation and encouragement.

Today's passage from Hebrews 4 allows us to understand better the results of Jesus' practice of servant leadership. As one who was like us in all things but sin, Jesus can be sympathetic toward us and can serve still as our advocate and defender. Because of his servant leadership, we can approach God confidently and even boldly, and expect to find mercy at what is now the "throne of grace." All this flows from and through the servant leadership of Jesus.

Praying with Scripture

How do you define leadership? Who best exemplifies leadership for you? Why?

In what respect is Jesus the best example of his own ideal of servant leadership?

Why does the author of Hebrews express the effects of Jesus' servant leadership in terms of sacrifice and priesthood? Do you find these images helpful? What images might you use?

Following Jesus on the Way
Thirtieth Sunday in Ordinary Time (B)

Readings: Jeremiah 31:7–9; Psalm 126:1–6; Hebrews 5:1–6; Mark 10:46–52

> Immediately he regained his sight and followed him
> on the way.
>
> —Mark 10:52

The journey with Jesus and his disciples from northern Galilee toward Jerusalem started with the healing of a blind man who only gradually came to see. Along the way we read some surprising texts about a suffering Messiah, greatness in the community of Jesus, tolerance toward outsiders of good will, the need to avoid scandal, fidelity in marriage, accepting God's kingdom as a gift, riches as a possible obstacle to happiness and salvation, and Jesus' ideal of servant leadership. At several points Jesus had to correct misunderstandings on the part of his closest followers.

Today's reading from the end of Mark 10 brings the journey nearer to a close. It is the story of the healing of another blind man, the beggar Bartimaeus. It takes place just as Jesus is leaving Jericho on the way to Jerusalem. In many respects this account is like other healing stories in Mark's Gospel. There is the physical problem of Bartimaeus's blindness. Bartimaeus displays a deep and persistent faith in Jesus' power to heal him. And the cure is immediate and complete.

The story of Bartimaeus also provides a model for all who follow Jesus on the way. His journey begins with a glimmer of faith, the hope that Jesus the Son of David can heal him. It grows with his plea, "Have mercy on me." When rebuked by others, he persists in calling on Jesus. When asked by Jesus what he wants, he expresses himself in the words of every would-be disciple: "My teacher, let me see again." And he comes to "see" on both physical and spiritual levels. His response to his healing is to follow Jesus "on the way." That way, of course, leads to Jerusalem, the place of Jesus' passion and death.

It is likely that both Mark's Gospel and the letter to the Hebrews were written in Rome within a few years of each another. Some scholars have perceived these two texts as complements of each other—Mark takes us up to Jesus' passion and death, and the author of Hebrews reflects on the theological significance of Jesus' passion, death, resurrection, and exaltation taken as a whole. Today's reading from Hebrews 5 develops further the themes of Jesus as the great high priest and the perfect sacrifice for sins.

The role of the Jewish high priest was to offer sacrifices to God and serve as a representative of the people. Jesus offered himself as a sacrifice for sins and continues to act as our mediator at "the throne of grace." The Jewish high priest was very much a human being, beset by weakness and sin. While no stranger to human weakness, Jesus the Son of God was able to deal compassionately with sinners without himself succumbing to sin. The appointment of the Jewish high priest was limited to men who could trace their ancestry to the tribe of Levi and to Aaron, the brother of Moses. Since Jesus was from the tribe of Judah rather than Levi, he could never act as the Jewish high priest while he was on earth. However, the author of Hebrews argues that Jesus the Son of God was appointed directly by God to an even better priesthood and quotes his two favorite Old Testament texts: "You are my son, today I have begotten you" (Psalm 2:7), and "You are a priest forever, according to the order of Melchizedek" (Psalm 110:4). And one of that author's favorite images of Jesus is that of the "pioneer of [our] salvation" (Hebrews 2:10; see also 12:2), the one who has gone on the way before us and cleared the path for us, thus making it possible to reach our goal in life—our heavenly home.

Today's reading from Hebrews reminds us that the way of Jesus does not end in Jerusalem. Jesus surpassed every high priest in ancient Israel. Through him we can approach the throne of grace with confidence and boldness, and we can expect mercy and favor from God. The way of Jesus leads to eternal life with God. He is indeed "the pioneer of [our] salvation" (Hebrews 2:10).

Praying with Scripture

In what respects is Bartimaeus's encounter with Jesus a model for prospective followers?

What did Bartimaeus come to see?

How would you describe "the way" of Jesus? What does it entail, and where does it lead?

Already and Not Yet

Thirty-Third Sunday in Ordinary Time (B)

Readings: Daniel 12:1–3; Psalm 16:5, 8–11; Hebrews 10:11–14, 18; Mark 13:24–32

> But about that day and hour no one knows, neither
> the angels in heaven, nor the Son, but only the Father.
>
> —Mark 13:32

At the close of one church year and the beginning of another, the Scripture readings lead us to consider "the last things," or what is often called *eschatology*. In the biblical context eschatology includes the resurrection of the dead, the Last Judgment, rewards and punishments, and the fullness of God's kingdom.

One way to grasp how the New Testament approaches last things is to use the terms *already* and *not yet*. Applying these terms to today's Scripture readings can help us understand a difficult topic and to reflect on how it might have an impact on the way we can think and live as Christians.

An excellent statement of what "already" means in New Testament eschatology comes in today's reading from Hebrews 10. There the author first contrasts the many sacrifices offered by Jewish high priests in the Jerusalem temple with the one perfect sacrifice offered by Jesus in his death on the cross. Whereas their repeated sacrifices failed to take away the sins of the people (otherwise they would not have kept offering them), "when Christ had offered for all time a single sacrifice for sins, 'he sat down at

the right hand of God.'" Most of Hebrews is an extended meditation on the significance of Jesus' death and resurrection for us. It
describes Jesus both as the perfect sacrifice for sins (perfect in that
it achieved its goal) and as the great High Priest (in that he willingly offered himself). His sacrifice made possible the forgiveness
of sins and a new relationship between God and humankind. This
new relationship is what we can enjoy through Christ *already*.

The "not yet" refers to the fact that the new relationship with
God through Jesus' death and resurrection represents the inauguration or anticipation of the future coming of God's kingdom in
its fullness. Paul used metaphors such as pledge, down payment,
and first fruits to describe the "already" dimension. He and the
other New Testament writers insisted that the fullness of God's
kingdom remains in the future as "not yet."

The "not yet" dimension is rooted in Jewish apocalyptic literature and is well illustrated by today's reading from the book
of Daniel, chapter 12. At the end of a long and detailed reflection on ancient Near Eastern history from the sixth to the
second centuries B.C., this short passage describes the "great
tribulation," the resurrection of the dead, and the divine judgment, with its rewards for the wise and righteous and its punishments for the foolish and wicked. This scenario includes
the earliest indisputable description of the resurrection of the
dead contained in the Old Testament. By the time of Jesus
and the New Testament writers, this scenario was taken for
granted in many Jewish circles. It underlies the "not yet" element in early Christian texts.

The "not yet" theme is also developed in today's se
from Mark 13, which is part of Jesus' eschatological disco
The text offers a picture of the end of the world as we know it and
of the Last Judgment. It uses images from various parts of the
Old Testament, especially from Daniel 7, to depict these events
and the coming of the Son of Man in glory. It also warns us to be
attentive to the signs of the so-called second coming of Jesus, and
ends with a reminder that no one knows its exact day or hour.

What does the "not yet" mean for us? How should it affect
our faith and lives? In Mark 13 and the other versions of Jesus'
eschatological discourse in Matthew 24—25 and Luke 21, the
apocalyptic scenario is followed by sayings and parables that urge
readers to be always on guard, vigilant, and watchful. We are to
act always as if the Son of Man were to come very soon. We are to
conduct ourselves always as if we were to face our judgment in the
next moment. This is not a stance of anxiety or fear. Rather, it is
a stance of hope, trust, and confidence that what God has begun
in Jesus' life, death, and resurrection—the "already"—God will
surely bring to a glorious completion in the future, the "not yet."

The terms *already* and *not yet* capture the New Testament
concept of "last things." Through Jesus' death and resurrection
we have already been freed from domination by sin and death
and freed for life in the Holy Spirit. We can now stand beside
Jesus and address God as "Our Father," as we look forward in
hope for the fullness of God's kingdom in the future. As we live
between the times of the "already" and the "not yet," we continue
to pray "Thy kingdom come!"

Praying with Scripture

How might you describe the "already" dimension of Christian life achieved through Jesus' life, death, and resurrection?

How literally do you take the apocalyptic scenarios in Daniel 12 and Mark 13? How do you understand them?

In what sense is the "Our Father" a prayer for the full coming of God's kingdom?

Readings from Mark's Gospel for Sundays and Feasts in the Year B

Sundays in Ordinary Time

1. 1:7–11
3. 1:14–20
4. 1:21–28
5. 1:29–39
6. 1:40–45
7. 2:1–12
8. 2:18–22
9. 2:23—3:6
10. 3:20–35
11. 4:26–34
12. 4:35–41
13. 5:21–43
14. 6:1–6
15. 6:7–13
16. 6:30–34
22. 7:1–8, 14–15, 21–23
23. 7:31–37
24. 8:27–35
25. 9:30–37

26. 9:38–43, 45, 47–48
27. 10:2–16
28. 10:17–30
29. 10:35–45
30. 10:46–52
31. 12:28–34
32. 12:38–44
33. 13:24–32

Other Feasts

Advent 1. 13:33–37
Advent 2. 1:1–8
Lent 1. 1:12–15
Lent 2. 9:2–10
Palm Sunday. 11:1–10
Passion Sunday. 14:1—15:47
Easter. 16:1–7
Ascension. 16:15–20
Body of Christ. 14:12–16, 22–26

For Further Reading

Byrne, Brendan J. *A Costly Freedom: A Theological Reading of Mark's Gospel.* Collegeville: Liturgical Press, 2008.

Collins, Adela Yarbro. *Mark: A Commentary.* Hermeneia. Minneapolis: Fortress, 2007.

Donahue, John R. and Daniel J. Harrington. *The Gospel of Mark.* Sacra Pagina 2. Collegeville: Liturgical Press, 2002; rev. ed., 2005.

Harrington, Daniel J. *What Are They Saying about Mark?* New York/Mahwah, NJ: Paulist, 2004.

Levine, Amy-Jill with Marianne Blickenstaff, eds. *A Feminist Companion to Mark.* Sheffield, UK: Sheffield Academic Press, 2001.

Marcus, Joel. *Mark 1–8; Mark 8–16.* Vols. 27 and 27A, Anchor Yale Bible. New Haven, CT: Yale University Press, 2002, 2009.

Moloney, Francis J. *The Gospel of Mark: A Commentary.* Peabody, MA: Hendrickson, 2002.

———. *Mark: Storyteller, Interpreter, Evangelist.* Peabody, MA: Hendrickson, 2004.

Reiser, William. *Jesus in Solidarity with His People: A Theologian Looks at Mark.* Collegeville: Liturgical Press, 2000.

Telford, William R. *The Theology of the Gospel of Mark.* New Testament Theology. Cambridge/New York: Cambridge University Press, 1999

About the Author

Daniel J. Harrington, SJ, is professor of New Testament at Boston College School of Theology and Ministry. He wrote "The Word" column for *America* magazine from 2005 to 2008. He has been writing an annual survey of recent "Books on the Bible" for *America* since 1984. Harrington has been editor of *New Testament Abstracts* since 1972 and served as president of the Catholic Biblical Association in 1985–86. He was a member of the official team for editing the Dead Sea Scrolls and focused on the wisdom texts from Qumran. He is also the editor of the Sacra Pagina commentary on the New Testament (Liturgical Press) to which he contributed the volumes on Matthew, Mark (with John Donahue), and 1 & 2 Peter and Jude (with Donald Senior). He has published extensively on the New Testament and on Second Temple Judaism. He is the author of *Meeting St. Paul Today* (2008), *Meeting St. Luke Today* (2009), and *Meeting St. Matthew Today* (2010), and *Meeting St. John Today* (2011), all published by Loyola Press.

Other books available in the *Meeting ... Today* series by Daniel J. Harrington, SJ

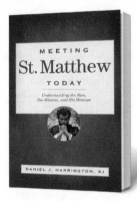

Meeting St. Matthew Today
$12.95 • 2914-5 • Paperback

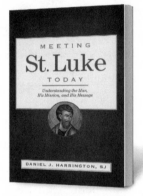

Meeting St. Luke Today
$12.95 • 2916-9 • Paperback

Meeting St. Paul Today
$12.95 • 2734-9 • Paperback

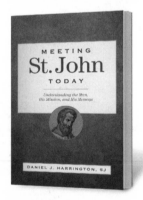

Meeting St. John Today
$12.95 • 2917-6 • Paperback

Enjoy all books in the *Meeting ... Today* series. Anytime. Anywhere.

All books in the *Meeting ... Today* series by Daniel J. Harrington, SJ, are now available as eBooks from Amazon, Barnes & Noble, Sony, Kobo, and Google. Visit your favorite eBook store to purchase these editions today.

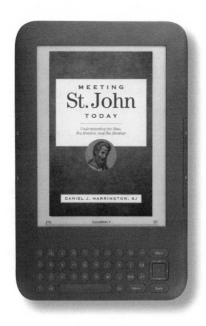

Six Weeks with the Bible

CATHOLIC PERSPECTIVES

Over 450,000 sold in the series!

This popular, award-winning series by Kevin Perrotta—
perfect for Bible-study groups as well as individual
study—helps lay Catholics understand Scripture and
apply it to their lives. The series includes 51 books
covering most of the New Testament, key Old Testament
texts, and important themes.

For a complete listing of titles, including Spanish titles
and titles written specifically for teens, please visit
www.loyolapress.com/six-weeks
or call 800-621-1008.

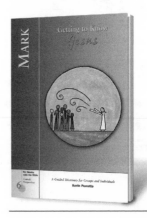